Crazy About Canada!

Maple Tree Press Inc.
51 Front Street East, Suite 200, Toronto, Ontario M5E 1B3
www.mapletreepress.com

Distributed in Canada by Raincoast Books
9050 Shaughnessy Street, Vancouver, British Columbia V6P 6E5

Distributed in the United States by Publishers Group West
1700 Fourth Street, Berkeley, California 94710

Cataloguing in Publication Data
Bowers, Vivien, 1951–

    Crazy about Canada! : amazing things kids want to know / Vivien Bowers ;
illustrated by Dianne Eastman.

(Canadian geographic kids)
Includes index.

ISBN 13: 978-1-897066-47-8 (bound) / ISBN 10: 1-897066-47-3 (bound)
ISBN 13: 978-1-897066-48-5 (pbk.) / ISBN 10: 1-897066-48-1 (pbk.)

1. Canada—Juvenile literature.
2. Canada—Miscellanea—Juvenile literature.
3. National characteristics, Canadian—Juvenile literature.
I. Eastman, Dianne   II. Title.   III. Series.

FC58.B678 2006   j971   C2005-904644-9

Design & art direction: Dianne Eastman
Illustrations: Dianne Eastman
Photo credits: see page 95

We acknowledge the financial support of the Canada Council for the Arts, the
Ontario Arts Council, the Government of Canada through the Book Publishing
Industry Development Program (BPIDP), and the Government of Ontario through
the Ontario Media Development Corporation's Book Initiative for our publishing
activities.

ONTARIO ARTS COUNCIL
CONSEIL DES ARTS DE L'ONTARIO

Printed in Hong Kong

B   C   D   E   F

Crazy About Canada!

AMAZING THINGS KIDS WANT TO KNOW

VIVIEN BOWERS

Illustrated by **DIANNE EASTMAN**

MAPLE TREE PRESS

Contents

Which Canadian school is closest to the North Pole? How many students go there?

I'm Vivien, and I'm off on a quest—an exciting search for truth! It's a research expedition to seek answers to incredible questions from kids across the country.

Hi, I'm Morton. I can see that Vivien is going to need my help.

NAME
NOM

What is slugs' slime made of?

Where in Canada does lightning strike most often?

Quest for Answers

When we asked kids like you from all across Canada to send in their very best questions about our country, they sure came through. We were flooded with questions!

Kids from Yahk to Fogo sent in hundreds and hundreds of questions about everything from polar bears to place names. So now these kids want answers. Challenge and adventure await!

Well, what's the hold up? Let's get started!

Morton, we'll have to be like detectives, sleuthing out the truth.

Sounds like dangerous work! I hope we don't get tangled in a maze of Websites in Cyberspace.

Why are beavers' teeth orange?

Are there poisonous snakes in Canada?

There were *loads* of questions about wildlife—polar bears, mosquitoes, moose, slugs, and more. So, wildlife seems like the best place to start uncovering some answers.

CHAPTER 1

Highly Questionable Critters

When you go researching, always leave a note saying where you're going, in case you get lost.

Brrr.... Bear?!

Plenty About Polar Bears

I'm doing swimmingly! I can go more than 100 km (60 mi.) without a rest.

How can polar bears swim in the cold Arctic water?

Nanook (that's the Inuit word for polar bear) is designed for polar dips. Being big helps it stay warm—there's a lot of warm-blooded animal inside that fur coat. The fur itself is double-layered. The outer layer is water repellent. And the hairs are hollow so they trap air and act as insulation. Under the woolly fur underwear there's a generous layer of blubber, adding further insulation and buoyancy. With all this protection, plus big paws for flippers, polar bears are champion cold-water swimmers.

Do polar bears freeze?

Polar bears' bodies are incredibly well insulated and adapted to cold. They may die of starvation, but if they have enough food they are not likely to freeze to death. A scientist once took an infrared photograph of a bear (infrared film shows where heat is given off) and it showed nothing except the puff of the bear's breath. The bear had almost no heat loss. On the worst winter days with bitterly cold winds, polar bears dig out a shelter in a snow drift and curl up into a ball to wait out the storm.

Where would I spot a polar bear roaming the streets of town?

Head to Churchill, Manitoba, on the shores of Hudson Bay. In the fall, you'll see bears roaming the streets there as they wait for the bay to freeze so they can go out on the ice and hunt seals. Most of Churchill's bears behave themselves, but threatening actions will land them in the town's polar bear "jail."

Are our polar bears dying out?

Thirty years ago, the world's five polar bear nations signed The International Agreement on the Conservation of Polar Bears. Since then, the number of bears has increased. Scientists figure there are between 22,000 and 25,000 polar bears in the world today—over half of them in Canada. But scientists are concerned because Arctic temperatures have been getting warmer. So in southern parts of the bears' range, such as Hudson Bay, the sea ice melts earlier in the spring, and freezes later in the fall. Without this ice, the bears can't get to their prey, the seals. If temperatures keep warming, and polar bears can't hunt for food, that Hudson Bay population of bears may not survive.

What is the largest polar bear ever found in Canada?

The largest weighed over 800 kg (1,765 lbs.). Don't let a bear that size step on your toes.

MORTON'S IRRESISTIBLE DETOUR

While we were researching the answers to your questions, we came across this fascinating polar bear fact about fat necks! Fat necks? Scientists track bears by attaching radio collars to them. As the bears roam, these radio transmitters send out signals that are picked up by satellites in space, then get relayed back to the scientists. But male polar bears have necks that are wider than their heads, so the radio collars slide off. The collars only stay on the females, so only female polar bears can be tracked.

What's that hairy thing?

It's my moosetache.

Moose on the Loose

How many moose live in Canada?

About one million moose live in North America, most of those in Canada. They are moosing their way into new territory that was previously moose-less. There are now moose in north-central Ontario and the southern part of British Columbia.

Are moose really Canadian?

Moose make an appearance on a special quarter that was given to all new Canadian citizens on Canada Day in 2004. The nifty design was done by 11-year-old Nick Wooster.

There's nothing uniquely "Canadian" about moose, but Canada has lots of them. Like most Canadians, the ancestors of today's moose came from someplace else. They came from Russia across the Bering land bridge that connected it to Alaska long ago. The descendants of those moose that didn't make the trip are still back there in the northern forests of Russia and Europe.

How much food does a moose eat?

Moose have big appetites. You would, too, if you weighed more than four refrigerators. In summer, they bulk up on a daily 25–30 kilograms (55–65 lbs.) of shrubs and other plants. In winter, moose eat 15–20 kilograms (35–45 lbs.) of twigs each day. Twigs take some digesting, which is why moose have four stomachs. Basically, they can regurgitate what they ate the first time to chew it some more. Charming.

MORTON'S IRRESISTIBLE DETOUR

Who came up with the name "moose?" The Algonquins called this creature *mooswa* (which is spelled in different ways) meaning "twig-eater" or "the animal that strips bark off trees." In Europe, they also have moose but call them "elk." Just to make this more confusing, North America also has elk, but they aren't the same as European elk (of course, because European elk are really moose). Europe does have the same animals that North Americans call elk, but in Europe they are called European red deer. (Are you keeping up?)

Why do moose have large antlers?

The better to fight with! Only bull moose (males) have antlers. Each year they grow a bigger rack. It can be a metre and a half (almost 5 ft.) across and weigh over 34 kilograms (75 lbs.)—about as much as you! The fuzzy skin on the antlers, called velvet, carries blood to the antlers. The blood deposits calcium, which is what antlers are made of.

Moose use the antlers during their autumn rut, when the bulls fight over who will mate with a female moose (cow). They circle and then bash their heads together. Usually they stop before anybody is badly hurt. This is nature's way of selecting only the strongest and healthiest moose to produce offspring.

Should we just call it a tie?

Sure, I've got a wicked headache.

HEAD-SCRATCHER

Why do moose have that hairy thing hanging under their chin?

That "thing" is called a dewlap, or a bell. Moose experts say that during mating season, a bull moose will make a wallow (a scooped-out hollow in the ground), pee in it, and then use his front feet to splash urine onto his dewlap and the underside of his antlers. The hairs on the dewlap actually stand out stiffly so that the urine can splash right down to the base of the hairs. The dewlap then gives off an odour ("eau de moose"?) that's irresistible to cow moose.

Why do moose lose their antlers in winter?

Would you carry that load on your head all winter? No way! After the rut, the bulls don't need those huge racks, so they drop them. They'll grow a new set the following summer.

13

Timber!

The Buzz on Beavers

Why do beavers build dams?

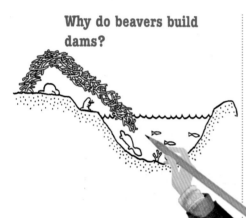

Clever beavers change their landscape to suit their needs. Their dams back up the water and create ponds. The beaver then builds a lodge with an underwater entrance, and the pond acts like a moat to repel predators like foxes, wolves, and coyotes. The dam raises the water level in the pond so it doesn't freeze in winter, giving the beaver year-round access. It swims into an entrance tunnel and climbs up out of the water into a safe, cozy chamber. When beavers run out of food around the pond, or the kits (baby beavers) are old enough to leave home, they move off to develop a new piece of prime beaver real estate.

Are beavers ever killed by the trees they fell?

Timber! CRASH! Logging is hazardous for both humans and rodents. Beavers log an average of 200 trees a year. They stand on their hind legs (using the tail for balance) and use their top front teeth to cut a ring around the tree trunk. Then they dig in their lower teeth below the ring to break out huge chips around the trunk. They are hard workers, but they don't seem to be able to aim the direction that their tree will fall. Occasionally, they don't get out of the way fast enough.

I give up!

You can't give up. Kids are depending on you to find the answer. I have an idea: On this wildlife Website, I can "Ask an Expert." I'll try that.

Why are beavers' teeth orange?

Orange you glad you finally found the answer?

Dear Expert: Why are beavers' teeth orange? Answer desperately required. Morton.

Dear Morton: They are orange because there's iron in the enamel coating on the front of the teeth. The iron makes the enamel hard. The back of the tooth doesn't have this hard coating. It's softer, so when it wears away, it leaves a hard, chisel-sharp biting edge.

How do beavers breathe underwater?

Here are some of my other under-water tricks.

They don't. Like you, they hold their breath, but they can hold it for 15 minutes. (Don't even try it.) Beavers have big lungs. Even if humans had lungs like that we couldn't hold our breath so long because our brains need oxygen. But the beaver has a pretty neat trick. It can divert blood (which carries the oxygen) from its paws to feed its brain.

Waterproof fur

Natural goggles (transparent membranes cover my eyes)

Automatic ear plugs

Automatic nose plugs (valves that close underwater)

Lips that close behind my teeth so I can carry sticks underwater

Why is the beaver a symbol of Canada?

Remember the fur trade? For about two hundred years, up until the mid-1800s, millions of Canadian beavers' pelts were shipped to Europe to make fancy beaver-skin hats. Because the beaver played such an important role in Canada's history and economy, it was often used as the country's symbol. In 1975, the beaver got the highest honour ever bestowed on a rodent when it became Canada's official emblem.

Make Way for Birds!

Honk! Honk! Honk! Honk! Honk! Honk! Honk! Honk! Honk! Honk! Honk!

Honk if you're crazy about Canada geese!

How far north do birds fly in Canada?

Ivory gulls have been seen flying over the North Pole in summer—that's as far north as it gets! Quttinirpaaq National Park is the most northerly place in Canada, at the tip of Ellesmere Island, Nunavut. With nine-month-long winters complete with 24-hour darkness, frequent blizzards, -40°C (-40°F) temperatures, and little food, no birds live there year-round. But come summer, about 30 species of birds nest in this land of midnight sun.

No one migrates like me—the Arctic tern. I migrate all the way from the Arctic to the Antarctic in the fall, then all the way back to the Arctic again in the spring. I'm an extreme migrator!

Why don't birds' feet freeze in winter?

Birds have tricks to avoid having their tootsies freeze in winter.
- Snowy owls and ptarmigans have fully feathered legs and feet— a practical fashion choice.
- The soles of owls' and ravens' feet have little, hard bumps that raise their feet off the cold ground and reduce heat loss.
- Some birds conserve heat by standing on one leg and bending the other up against the belly; others sit on the ground with both legs covered by the body.
- Seabirds and waterfowl usually have wet feet—brrrrrr! But these talented birds can cool their feet almost to the freezing point, while warm blood flows through the rest of their bodies, keeping them warm.

What is the difference between a raven and a crow?

I'm the raven. I have a wedge-shaped tail. And I'm bigger.

Raven

Crow

Well, don't crow about it, because I'm the crow.

Do we yield right-of-way to jumbo jets?   That might be prudent.   Did we file a flight plan?   Where's the first marsh stop?

Are we there yet?

Canada geese migrating.

Why do some Canada geese fly south for the winter while others stay?

Winter approaches. Some birds just fluff up their feathers (instant down jacket) and hunker down for the winter. Others migrate, either a short or long way. Why? It comes down to food. When the snow falls and the lakes and rivers freeze over in Canada's north, most Canada geese take to the flyways. Some just migrate from northern to southern Canada—to where the ponds and rivers don't freeze and there's plant food to eat. Most honk their way farther south to the United States and Mexico. But some Canada geese don't migrate at all. They've discovered that the gobbling is good on the grassy parks and golf courses that humans have built. There may also be leftover grain in nearby fields, and sometimes people even bring them bird seed. There's no place like home for the holidays!

To V or not to V— that is the question.

MORTON'S IRRESISTIBLE DETOUR

Ever wondered why geese fly in a V-formation? I did. This is what I found out: It's less effort, for one thing. There's less air resistance. It's like in a bicycle race, where one rider takes the lead while the others conserve energy by staying just behind in the "draft." A V-shape also makes it easier for all the geese to follow the leader because they can see what's happening ahead. If the leader decides to change direction or speed, that information can be quickly communicated to all members of the flock.

Aaaack! Attack!

How many animals in Canada attack people?

Bears (black bears, grizzlies, and polar bears), wolves, and cougars have all attacked people. But get real—the chance of you being attacked by these wild animals is incredibly small. You are more likely to be killed by a bee. (Now don't start worrying about bees!)

How do I avoid a cougar attack?

Cougars are stealth attackers. They sneak up from behind and leap on the neck of their prey (a deer, for instance) hoping to break its neck. If that doesn't work, their teeth are designed to sever the jugular vein with a bite across the throat. Sounds scary, but there's really no need to worry. Cougar attacks on people are very, very rare. Most happen on Vancouver Island, but even there they are very uncommon. The big cats are so elusive, few people ever get to see one in the wild.

If you know that there are cougars in the area, here are some good tips to avoid an encounter with a cougar. (Many of them are the same as for bears.)

- hike in groups of two or more; stay near the adults because cougars rarely attack bigger people
- make noise to prevent surprising a cougar
- never approach a cougar
- if you see one, don't panic and run; be calm, back away (face the cat—don't turn your back), and give it room to escape
- if ever attacked, fight back; don't play dead

Are there poisonous snakes in Canada?

I just encountered a human—that was scary! Now I'm a little rattled!

There's only one poisonous snake in Canada: the rattlesnake. It has more right to be scared of you than you are of it. Rattlesnakes are shy loners and prefer to stay hidden. But when they emerge into the sun to soak up some rays, they sometimes meet people. Due to hunters bent on exterminating "dangerous" rattlesnakes, there are nowhere near as many snakes as there used to be. Rattlers need more friends. (But not "close friends"—keep your distance.)

How many grizzly bear attacks have there been?

Here's a tip to avoid a bear encounter: Make a lot of noise to warn bears of your approach. How's your singing?

There are about 60,000 grizzlies in North America, along with 900,000 black bears. There are millions of meetings between people and bears each year. Yet only about 3 people per year in North America die from bear attacks, and 12 are seriously injured. Grizzlies are responsible for most of the attacks, even though there are far fewer of them. But all bears generally prefer to avoid people.

Grizzly bear

This land is your land,
This land is my land....

Here he comes again! I can barely stand it.

You think his singing is bad; you should hear him on the tuba!

Stephen Herrero

Interview with Stephen Herrero, author of Bear Attacks: Their Causes and Avoidance.

Vivien: You're a biologist, and you study animal behaviour. But why bear attacks?

Steve Herrero: In 1967, two young women were killed by grizzly bears in Glacier National Park in two separate events. People were shocked. This was the first time anyone had been killed by a bear in the park. One biologist suggested all grizzlies in the park should be shot. I decided that somebody like me ought to collect accurate records of bear attacks and learn more about bear behaviour.

Vivien: Does that mean learning to think like a bear?

Steve Herrero: Yes. And the more I learn, the more complex bear behaviour appears. There's a quote in my book, "If a lion could talk, we probably couldn't understand him." It's meant to show how complex the world of any animal is.

Vivien: What's a common misunderstanding?

Steve Herrero: People think bears attack unpredictably, at random. But if you take time to know bears, their behaviour is actually quite predictable. For each species of bear, there are sets of circumstances that can lead to an attack. For a grizzly, it's usually a mother defending her cubs. Also, individual bears have their own personalities. When you come to know them as individuals, their behaviour is as predictable as human beings'.

Vivien: And we all know about THEM!

On the Slime Trail

How did slugs get their name?

Is it because "slug" rhymes with "ugh?"

Shift your time machine into reverse; go back about 600 years. At that time, people used the word *slugge* or *sluggi* to describe folks who were lazy, slothful, or slow. (Today we'd say they were sluggish.) Then about 300 years ago, the word slug started being applied to a slow-moving, shell-less land snail, presumably because it was rather sluggish.

Why are there huge banana slugs on the west coast?

Slugs like it wet. Their eggs won't even hatch if it's too dry. So the wet west coast is slug paradise. That's where you find enormous banana slugs. (N.B. Do NOT try making banana smoothies from banana slugs!) Other species of slugs have adapted to living far from the coast, so scout around in shady, damp areas...and watch where you step!

What is slugs' slime made of?

What's this poster, Morton? A plug for slugs?

That's a sticky question! Scientists wish they knew what was in slug slime. They've tried to reproduce it because slime is a great natural glue with many possible uses. For instance, it could be used in medicine to coat wounds so they wouldn't dry out.

Give a slug a hug!

Maybe we could stick it up with slug slime.

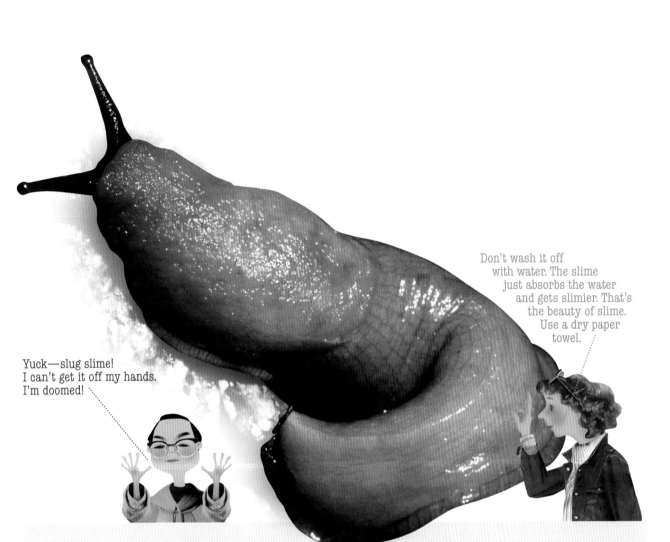

Yuck—slug slime!
I can't get it off my hands.
I'm doomed!

Don't wash it off
with water. The slime
just absorbs the water
and gets slimier. That's
the beauty of slime.
Use a dry paper
towel.

SPECIAL REPORT: SLUG SLIME

Slug slime is wonderful, amazing stuff. It's similar to what oozes from your nose when you have a cold, but much more useful. Here's how:

· It keeps slugs from drying out. Their coating of slime acts like a sponge, absorbing water from the air and the soil. In hot, dry weather, slugs just curl up in a blanket of slime until the next fog or rain.

· Slime is also a gooey defense against predators. When threatened, slugs turn themselves into big slime balls. Most animals and birds find that the slimy stuff tastes disgusting, so they're not interested.

· Slime also gets slugs where they want to go. The goo provides a slippery trail across the forest floor. The slime trail protects the animal's soft, mushy body from sharp objects. Snails and slugs can actually glide across sharp razor blades without cutting themselves! What's more, they use slime to help them stick to steep surfaces or plant stems, and even hang upside down from slime threads.

· Slime is useful in mating too. A slug that is ready to find a mate leaves a chemical in the slime to attract other slugs. Another slug smells the chemical and follows the trail of slime to the slug that left it.

Brrrr! These questions make me shiver. Maybe I'll crawl into a cozy hole and (yawn) hibernate for a while. Zzzzzzz....

No, don't fall asleep! Lots of kids want to know how creepy-crawlies survive the winter.

Cold-Blooded in Winter

Do ants hibernate in the winter?
Why don't spiders freeze to death?
What do snakes do during winter?
Where do butterflies go when the snow comes?
What happens to earthworms in the winter?

Okay, okay. You probably already know that cold-blooded creatures aren't like warm-blooded ones. They can't keep warm when the air around them is cold. They cool down too. That makes them slow and sluggish. Sluggish is okay, but they sure don't want to freeze to death! So they've come up with a number of clever survival tricks.

Trick No. 1: Go Undercover

Many creatures hide out for the winter some place where it doesn't freeze, like deep in the soil, under piles of leaves, inside a rotting log, or under the bark of a tree. Some insects are protected inside cocoons. Others are in hard pupal cases. They will hatch out in the spring. Worms wriggle deep into the soil below the frost line. So what happens in the Arctic, where there is little soil? There are no earthworms!

Trick No. 2: Head for Some Place Warm

Some insects migrate to warmer climates for the winter. Monarch butterflies are famous for their annual flight to their favourite trees in Mexico. Other insects just migrate to more protected habitat nearby, or sneak into your warm basement. Greetings, spiders!

Trick No. 3: Live off Body Fat until Spring

If cold-blooded critters, such as ants, aren't doing much, they don't need a lot of food. By not looking for food, they don't use up energy. Their stored fat will keep them going until the weather warms up again—handy because there's not much food around in winter anyway.

Heading to Mexico again this winter?

You bet!

Caribou

Winter is a tricky time to be a snake. If I freeze, I'll die. So snakes snuggle up in a winter den called a hibernaculum—a hole in the rocks, an ant mound, or an underground burrow.

zzz
zzzz
zzz
zzz

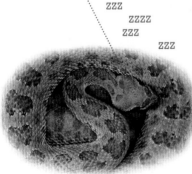

Trick No. 4: Hole Up Inside Someone Else's Warm Body
For instance, there's a fly that lays eggs on caribou hairs. The eggs hatch and the fly larvae (maggots) burrow into the caribou and spend the winter under its skin. A caribou may carry around 2,000 maggots.

Trick No. 5: Dry Up
Ice crystals forming in an insect's cells can be deadly. So some insects partially dehydrate their cells (forcing water out of them). That makes them less likely to freeze.

Trick No. 6: Slow Down and Snooze—A Lot
To save energy, many animals slow down their heart rate, breathing, and growth. They become dormant. It's like they put their lives on "pause" until the days grow longer and warmer again.

Trick No. 7: Freeze and Thaw
Some critters actually freeze in the winter, then thaw out and carry on with their lives in spring. Some insects produce a sort of antifreeze that prevents their bodies from freezing in sub-zero temperatures.

Mine, too.

Hey, what's bugging you?
Come back!

Record-Breaking Animals

Which is the biggest bird in Canada?

The Contestants:

Bald Eagles are Canada's biggest birds of prey.

Whooping Cranes are Canada's tallest birds, thanks to their long, slender legs. And their wingspan, tip to tip, can reach 2 metres (6 1/2 ft.) or more.

Trumpeter Swans are Canada's largest waterfowl. Large males can weigh 12 kilograms (26 lbs.). Play the trumpet fanfare!

American White Pelicans have an even bigger wingspan than whooping cranes— up to 3 metres (10 ft.).

Pull your head out of the sand, birdbrains. Ostriches are by far the biggest bird in Canada.

TWEET!
Disqualification!
Ostriches are not native to Canada!

What is the tiniest bug in Canada?

Meet a tiny, feather-winged beetle called *Nanosella fungi*. It's smaller than the period at the end of this sentence.

What's the biggest water turtle in Canada?

The leatherback is the *world's* largest living turtle—over 2 metres (6 ½ ft.) long and weighing 900 kilograms (1,985 lbs.). That's more than a moose! Leatherbacks are champion deep-sea divers. Although it usually lives in warmer waters to the south, the leatherback has occasionally been found swimming in the Gulf of St. Lawrence or off the coast of British Columbia. So it counts as Canadian, right?

What's the longest-living animal in Canada?

The blue whale scores there. It's the longest-living animal, with a normal lifespan of 60 to 80 years—and sometimes even up to 100! It also has the longest tongue, and—are you ready for this? (cover your ears)—it's the LOUDEST! The blue whale's call can be heard hundreds of kilometres away, louder than a jet plane.

Does Canada have the biggest mosquitoes?

Yes, indeed! Monster, blood-sucking varmints! The biggest, blood-suckingest mosquito in the world is probably *Psorophora ciliata*, also known as the feather-legged gallinipper. According to an expert on mosquitoes, a gallinipper bite is truly painful! (Note to self: remember not to become an expert on mosquitoes.) We do indeed have these nasty critters in Canada. But the swarms of mosquitoes that can make our lives miserable in Canada's north are actually a smaller species. There are over 2,500 different species of mosquitoes throughout the world.

Talk about big mosquitoes! Check out this giant! It was sighted in Komarno, Manitoba, north of Winnipeg. (Incidentally, *komar* is the Slovak word for mosquito.)

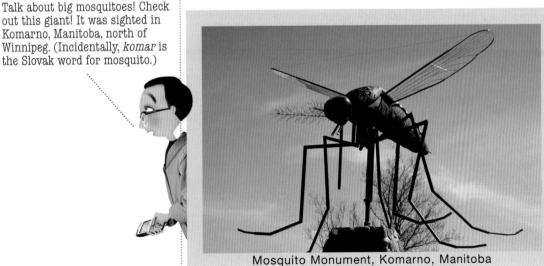

Mosquito Monument, Komarno, Manitoba

Yo, inchworm!

What Lives Where, and Why?

What animals are found only in Canada?

During the ice ages thousands of years ago, most of Canada was covered by huge glaciers. Those ice sheets either got rid of all the animals or pushed them south. Since that time, Canada has been re-populated with animals from other parts of the world. That means these animals aren't uniquely Canadian. There hasn't been enough time for new and different animal species to evolve in Canada.

I'm an exception. I'm the Vancouver Island marmot and I only live on Vancouver Island, where there are places that weren't covered by glaciers during the last ice ages.

Why are marmots found only in British Columbia?

Although the Vancouver Island marmot lives only on Vancouver Island, Canada has other marmots that do live outside of B.C. Hoary marmots live in the mountains of British Columbia *and* the Alberta Rockies. Another marmot, better known as a woodchuck or groundhog, is found all across Canada. Yes, the furry critter that sticks its nose out of its burrow every Groundhog Day is actually a marmot.

How much wood would a woodchuck chuck...?

Bobcat | Lynx | Cougar

Cougars have long tails. Do not, however, catch a cougar by the tail.

How many big cats live in Canada?

These are the big three: bobcat, lynx, and cougar. The lynx and bobcat look quite similar and have stubby tails, but the lynx has bigger feet. Those big feet make dandy snowshoes. The cougar is the biggest cat. Cougars are common only in western Canada these days.

Should we be called inchworms here? I thought Canada used metric units!

Good point! How about "2.54 centimetre worms?"

Are there inchworms in Canada?

Sure, you'll find inchworms here. Inchworms are the larvae of moths. Have you ever watched how an inchworm inches its way along? The worm has foot pads at either end of its body. It starts by sticking down the foot pads at its rear end. Then it extends its body forward and attaches the front end. Then it brings the rear part forward to meet the front part. It never lets go—there is always some part holding on tight. Mechanical engineers have studied the inchworm's loopy method of locomotion to make machines that move like that.

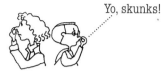
Yo, skunks!

What Else Lives Where, and Why?

Why are there no stinky skunks in Newfoundland?

Don't bother looking for us skunks in Newfoundland. You'll be skunked.

There are no skunks, no porcupines, no raccoons, no groundhogs, no deer, no snakes, and no end of other missing critters and plants in Newfoundland. The glaciers that covered the island during the ice ages pretty much wiped it clean of plants and animals. The island had to re-stock from Canada's mainland. Insects and birds flew across, and beavers swam. Some animals such as coyotes walked across the sea ice that forms in winter. But animals like skunks and snakes that hibernate, or just stay close to home in winter, didn't make the crossing.

How did moose get on the island of Newfoundland?

Like most folks, they arrived by boat. It's too far for a moose to swim! A hundred years ago, two pairs (four moose) were brought to the island. Those moose had calves. Then those calves grew up and had more calves. There are no wolves on Newfoundland to keep moose numbers under control. So there are now multitudinous moosies, all descendants of those first two pairs.

Where do bats live in Canada?

In caves, belfries, and other spots they hang out, you'll find bats of one kind or another almost everywhere in this country. Thank them, for they gobble up mosquitoes.

I'm a hoary bat—the biggest of the bats. My wingspan is 40 centimetres (15 ½ in.).

Are there reindeer in Canada?

Sure, because reindeer are really caribou. We are the same species. People in Europe and Asia tend to call us "reindeer" while North Americans call us "caribou."

Why are there no wolves in Nova Scotia?

Predators like wolves go where there's a dependable source of prey, like caribou and moose. But in Nova Scotia, the caribou and moose populations yo-yo up and down. So the wolves don't stay. With no wolves, the moose population booms until there are way too many of the long-nosers. They all browse on trees and shrubs, eventually decimating their habitat. Then the moose population crashes because there's not much to eat. It takes a long time for the population to recover. All these ups and downs—it's a roller-coaster ride in Nova Scotia!

Why do penguins live at the South Pole and not at the North Pole?

They can't get to the North Pole! Near the South Pole, cold ocean currents produce the fish feast penguins need to survive. A current carries chilly Antarctic water all the way up the coast of South America to the equator, so penguins have travelled as far north as the Galapagos Islands. But they can't go much farther. There's the cold water they need at the North Pole, but the little guys in tuxedos can't cross the warmer water in between, and they don't fly. A penguin was once sighted this far north—off the coast of British Columbia—but it was an escapee from a nearby zoo!

The North Pole may not have penguins but it has us—auks. We're expert divers, using our wings to swim underwater.

29

See any whales, Morton?

Why Do They Act Like That?

These guys are Canada's rock jocks.

Mountain goat

Mountain sheep

How do mountain sheep climb mountains?

Check out their climbing boots. The cloven (two-part) hoofs have a hard rim around the outer edge. Inside, the foot pads are roughened to provide better traction on the rocks. Mountain sheep are second only to mountain goats at scaling the high peaks. Sheep have strong hind legs that propel them up steep slopes. They cross cliff faces on the narrowest of ledges. From on high, the sheep have a good view of any approaching predators such as wolves, coyotes, or grizzly bears that might want to scoop up a tasty lamb. About the only predators that can reach them up there are mountain lions, wolverines, and golden eagles.

Why do whales grow super-sized?

On land, an animal's legs would collapse under too much weight. But in the ocean, the water helps support this weight. So whales can grow big. Blue whales grow biggest of all, over 100 tonnes. That's as much as 20 elephants. Being super-sized has advantages. It's easier to stay warm in the cold polar oceans where the whales feed. Big whales also store lots of fat in their blubber to last them when they don't get as much to eat. A big whale may eat five times its weight in food in a year. That's a lot of food, but you probably eat 15 times your weight in a year.

Why do lemmings follow each other over cliffs and fall in the ocean?

Down with misleading Hollywood movies about lemmings!

That's a myth! It was started by a 1958 Disney movie called *Wild Wilderness*, filmed in Alberta. Filmmakers brought in lemmings from the Arctic. They shot dramatic footage of the lemmings being released and herded over a cliff into a river. People thought it was a real event. So now, when crowds of people foolishly follow each other, we say they are acting like lemmings. That's unfair to lemmings! Lemmings don't follow each other over cliffs and they usually avoid water. In fact, most lemmings in Canada's north live on flat land, far from the ocean.

HEAD-SCRATCHER

How do groundhogs see underground?

Great question! Since groundhogs are a type of marmot, we went to a marmot expert to answer this one. According to Dr. Marmot, these burrowing rodents actually don't see well in the dark. So they probably feel their way around the tunnels and chambers of their underground burrow. He suggested you imagine trying to feel your way along a very narrow hallway, with only a few narrow rooms off to the side. But, unlike you, marmots have very sensitive whiskers that help them navigate.

Uh-oh. Palaeontologist tracks...

Dinosaurus Mysteriosus

Where did dinosaurs live in Canada?

At least it's fossilized so it doesn't smell bad.

Coprolite

We only know where dinosaurs lived when they left behind clues—fossilized dinosaur bones, footprints in hardened mud, nests, and coprolites (that's fossilized dinosaur poop).

Alberta, in particular, is world-famous for dinosaur fossils. Bones have even been discovered within two Alberta cities, Edmonton and Grand Prairie, and who knows how many more lurk beneath roads and parking lots. Dinosaur remains have also been found in smaller numbers in Saskatchewan, British Columbia, Nova Scotia, Yukon, Northwest Territories, and Nunavut. Dinosaurs probably lived in other places in Canada too. Maybe even in your backyard!

That's definitely a good thing.

Have dinosaurs' remains ever been found in the Arctic or Antarctic?

Yes to both. But that doesn't mean dinosaurs once had frozen noses and toes. The Earth's continents have drifted since the time of the dinosaurs 230 to 65 million years ago. Back then, land that's now in the Arctic was situated much farther south. The climate was more dinosaur-friendly, with trees and lush plants. On Bylot Island, off the northern tip of Baffin Island, a palaeontologist has found foot bones and teeth from a 70-million-year-old tyrannosaurid. It would have been almost 11 metres (36 ft.) long. The lower jaw of a hadrosaur (duckbill dinosaur) had earlier been found on the same island. As for Antarctica, during the time of the dinosaurs it was still attached to Australia. That combined land mass was slowly drifting south from the equator. Many animals lived there, including dinosaurs. Much later, after the dinosaurs were extinct, Antarctica broke off from Australia and drifted to its current chilly position at the South Pole.

I'm an *Albertosaurus*. You think I was big and nasty? You should meet my cousin *T. rex!*

MORTON'S IRRESISTIBLE DETOUR

Wet Science: In 2001, Daniel Helm, 9, and Mark Turner, 11, were tubing through rapids near Tumbler Ridge, British Columbia. When Mark fell out of his tube, the two boys headed for shore. And there they discovered dinosaur tracks that turned out to be those of an ankylosaur. Further excavation revealed bones at the site, only the second time dinosaur bones had been discovered in B.C.! Way to go, young dino hunters!

Mark Turner

Daniel Helm

Ka-Boom!

Why did dinosaurs die?

The most popular theory is that 65 million years ago a massive asteroid from space slammed into the Earth, creating a global dust cloud that blotted out the sun. Plants died and temperatures dropped below freezing for months or even years, causing mass extinctions. Other theories for the end of the dinosaurs include ongoing volcanic eruptions, climate change, habitat change as shallow inland seas dried up, or a combination of factors.

So, dino, want to help us solve this mystery once and for all? Which is the true extinction theory?

I don't think he's talking.

On the Edge of Extinction

What animals and birds are extinct in Canada today?

Here are some that have become extinct just in the past 100 years or so. (Of course, dinosaurs and other animals faced extinction long before that.) There's a little caribou that lived only on Haida Gwaii (the Queen Charlotte Islands, B.C.) and that went extinct in the 1920s. The last sea mink on the Atlantic coast died in 1894. The penguin-like great auk once gathered in large breeding colonies on rocky coasts of the Atlantic Ocean. After years of over-hunting, the last ones were killed by collectors in 1844. Another sea bird, the Labrador duck, also went extinct around 1875. Passenger pigeons once flew in flocks so enormous they blocked out the sun. Billions of them lived in North America. Slaughtered for their meat, they were virtually wiped out by 1890. The last survivor died in captivity in 1914.

QUEEN CHARLOTTE ISLANDS CARIBOU

SEA MINK

PASSENGER PIGEON

GREAT AUK

LABRADOR DUCK

What are the rarest or most endangered animals in Canada?

Black-footed ferret

Vancouver Island marmot

Northern spotted owl

The black-footed ferret is so rare in Canada you'll find it only in zoos. These furry, weasel-like animals used to live on Canada's prairie grasslands. Their favourite food was prairie dogs. As farms took over the grasslands, those burrowing prairie dogs were considered a nuisance so they were poisoned and hunted down. When they disappeared, the ferrets died out too. Today, black-footed ferrets bred in captivity have been reintroduced to grassland habitats in the United States. We can't introduce them to Canada until we have a healthy population of prairie dogs for them to eat.

The rarest animal still found in the wild in Canada is probably the Vancouver Island marmot. It lives only on some high mountains on Vancouver Island in British Columbia. The number of wild marmots dropped to only about a dozen. Scientists are raising other marmots at zoos, hoping they can later be released into their natural habitat to boost the population.

The northern spotted owl lives only in old growth forests. In Canada, that habitat is found along the southern coast of British Columbia. We've been logging these ancient trees, so the owls are now endangered.

I'm a prairie dog. I'm not actually a dog, but I am what the black-footed ferret likes to eat. I think he should eat broccoli instead.

DANGER SCALE

Hold fire! Stop that subdivision! In the past, over-hunting was usually the reason animals became scarce or even extinct. Today it's loss of their habitat. As people construct houses and roads, cut down forests, and turn wilderness into farms, the amount of habitat left for wildlife shrinks.

EXTINCT

"Extinct" means the animal no longer exists. It's gone forever.

EXTIRPATED

"Extirpated" means that this animal no longer lives in the wild in Canada. It still lives in other countries or in captivity.

ENDANGERED

"Endangered" means that this species is in big trouble, facing imminent extirpation or extinction.

THREATENED

"Threatened" is not quite as bad as endangered, but these animals still need our help.

So many Canada geese were hunted a hundred years ago, we were in big trouble!

Sounds like a wild goose tale!

Actually, it's true. But as you can see, they've recovered.

Back from the Brink

What animals have we saved from extinction?

Whooping crane

Peregrine falcon

Pronghorn

Swift fox

At one time whooping cranes were down to only 15 birds in North America—yikes! Now a couple hundred of these birds exist in the world. They face the most danger during their migration from nesting sites in Wood Buffalo National Park (along the border between Alberta and the Northwest Territories) to wintering grounds in the southern United States. Biologists are trying to start a second, migratory flock of whooping cranes. The cranes are hatched from eggs laid in captivity. So that the birds don't get used to humans, people dress in white costumes and use crane hand puppets. When it's time to migrate, an ultralight aircraft leads the way until the birds learn the route themselves.

Peregrine falcons are the fastest birds on the planet. That didn't help them when they started dying at an alarming rate in the 1950s. Scientists discovered that they were being poisoned, especially by an insecticide called DDT, sprayed on crops to kill insects. Small birds gobbled the poisoned seeds and insects, and those birds in turn were eaten by the peregrines. Because of the DDT in their bodies, peregrines started laying thin-shelled eggs that cracked before the chicks could hatch. Fortunately DDT has been banned. Peregrines are still endangered in some areas, but thousands of birds were bred in captivity and released to help bring the peregrine back from the brink of extinction.

For millions of years, pronghorns, North America's fastest animals, ranged across deserts and grasslands from Mexico to Canada. Then their habitat was taken over by farms. By the 1920s, pronghorn numbers were plummeting. They recovered when people stopped hunting them and began restoring farmland to pronghorn habitat.

The little swift fox disappeared from Canada's Prairies during the early 1900s. They still existed in the United States, so starting in the 1970s, swift foxes were captured down there and reintroduced to southern Alberta and Saskatchewan. Welcome back, little doggie.

Why is the St. Lawrence beluga whale in trouble?

There were once about 5,000 belugas in the Gulf of St. Lawrence near the mouth of the Saguenay River. Now there are fewer than 500. Belugas are actually supposed to live in cold Arctic oceans. The St. Lawrence group got trapped much farther south at the end of the ice ages, 10,000 years ago. They survived because icy water from the bottom of the St. Lawrence gets pushed up to the surface here, so it's like a mini Arctic ocean. Lots of plankton live in that cold water, and they attract the fish that make up the beluga's diet. That's why belugas have survived in the St. Lawrence. But it's not such a great place to hang out anymore. One big reason is that the St. Lawrence River is polluted with toxic chemicals—pollution from cities, factories, and farms—that make the whales sick. We'd better clean up our act!

Beluga whale

We're Web Spiders—special computer programs that Search Engines use to find information on the Internet.

Let's say you want to find out about the oldest maple tree in Canada. You can focus your search by using these Keywords: "oldest maple tree" + Canada.

The quotation marks tell us to search for those words all together. Using a plus sign (+) or the word "and" says you want both words or phrases ("oldest maple tree" and Canada) included in your search.

Oops, Morton! Looks like you got caught in the World Wide Web.

It was an accident. I did an Internet search and got 750,392,223,904 matches.

CHAPTER 2

Where does all the water come from that flows over Niagara Falls?

How far north do trains go?

These questions are about places and things in Canada—borders, mountains, rivers, and rainbows. Prepare to do some virtual travelling.

This Land of Ours: Top to Bottom and Inside Out

Time to measure Canada, Morton.

We are going to need a *really* long tape measure.

TOFINO

ST. JOHN'S

Canada on the Map

How big is Canada?

- It's 9,984,670 square kilometres (3,855,383 sq. mi.), including lakes and rivers.
- It's the second largest country in the world (after Russia).
- It's big enough to accommodate 26 Japans, 23 Iraqs, or 5 Mexicos within its borders.

I wonder how long it would take to dig my way across Canada?

Let's see.... That means, according to my calculations, that Canada is larger than *6 billion* NHL hockey rinks!

How do you measure the distance of the coastline of a big country like Canada?

Maps are digitized these days (put into a computer) and software programs can measure lines on the map. Canada has the longest coastline of any country in the world. (The coastline officially includes the coasts of all the offshore islands.) The total length is 202,080 kilometres (125, 570 mi.). Stretched out, that's equivalent to 25 times around the Earth's equator.

We found out there's a Web cam set up at the North Pole so you can see what's happening there! Check it out at http://www.arctic.noaa.gov and click on the Gallery.

North Pole

Is the North Pole in Canada?

Yes, sort of. There's actually no land at the North Pole—just a bunch of ice floating on the ocean, which is about 4,000 metres (13,120 ft.) deep at that spot. The Canadian government says its territory extends to the North Pole. The borders of Canada become closer and closer together, like a piece of pizza, until they come to a point at the tip— that's the North Pole (see page 68).

Are there still parts of Canada that haven't been discovered yet?

Thanks to satellite and aerial photographs, there's no part of Canada that we haven't seen from the air. But there are certainly places where nobody has set foot. These spots are usually hard to get to. They aren't on rivers or natural transportation routes; they aren't worth exploring for minerals or other natural resources; they don't have big tourist attractions. There's no reason for anyone to go there—except to find some place where nobody has ever gone. You could probably find an unexplored place on one of the Arctic islands in Canada's Far North. Or perhaps a swampy spot on the Canadian Shield. Or deep in the boreal (northern) forest. Don't forget your compass if you go exploring!

Roller-Coaster Canada

**Which province has the
highest ski slope?**

Alberta wins. Sunshine Village in the Alberta Rockies currently has
the highest ski slope (top elevation is 2,700 metres/8,858 ft.). But
not for long: ski hills planned in British Columbia will be even higher.

**How were the Rocky and
the Laurentian mountain
chains formed?**

Warning:
This answer
contains scenes
of violence.

The Earth's crust is made of gigantic tectonic plates that slowly drift
around like chunks of ice on a lake. When two plates collide, or one
gets rammed under the other, a lot of squishing and scrunching
happens at the edges. Rock gets thrust upwards—thousands of
metres—to form scenic mountains along the crash line. Both the
Laurentians in Quebec and the Rockies out west were formed from
plate collisions at different times.

HEAD-SCRATCHER

**What is the oldest
mountain in
Canada?**

Tricky question! You see, the older a mountain is, the more
likely it is to be worn down until it's not a mountain anymore.
Some of Canada's oldest mountains are long gone. Luckily, the
Laurentian Mountains north of Quebec City still have peaks over
1,000 metres (3,280 ft.) high. The Laurentians are one of the oldest
mountain ranges in the world, made of rock that's over 544 million years old.

**Why are the Rocky
Mountains so tall?**

The Rockies are just youngsters, geologically speaking. They're only
65 million years old. They haven't been around long enough to be worn
down by wind, water, and ice. Many peaks are still over 3,000 metres
(9,840 ft.) tall. By contrast, Quebec's Laurentian Mountains, which
were once just as high and mighty, have shrunk. And the Appalachian
Mountains in the Maritime provinces, formed about 400 million years
ago, have been smoothed down to scenic bumps. Canada's youngest,
highest peaks are the St. Elias Mountains in the Yukon, and they are
still growing! Deep down, one of Earth's plates is ramming in underneath the edge of another, jacking up the mountains.

Why are the Prairies so flat?

Millions of years ago, the Prairies were covered by huge, shallow seas. Over the years, layers of mud and silt settled to the bottom. That silty sea bottom has become today's flat and rolling prairie landscape. It's easy to see how flat the Prairies are because of the lack of trees. There used to be trees, but after the Rocky Mountains began to rise, the mountains blocked rainstorms coming in from the west. So the Prairies became too dry for trees—and desert plants and grasses moved in.

45

Here, get out of the rain!

Get the Weather Picture

Where in Canada does lightning strike most often?

Thank you. That was very enlightening.

The hotspots are southern Ontario, southern Saskatchewan (near Estevan), and the foothills of Alberta (west of Edmonton). The most zapped cities are Windsor, Toronto, Hamilton, Kitchener, and London—all in southern Ontario. Next on the list is Regina, Saskatchewan. If you don't like lightning, then head north to Inuvik, Whitehorse, or Yellowknife.

What is the foggy haze over water in winter?

Steam fog, a.k.a. evaporation fog or sea smoke (when it's over salt water), is the haze that forms when cold air flows over warmer water. Before the cold air arrives, the air sitting on the surface of a pond, lake, or ocean is about the same temperature as the water. When it mixes with incoming cold air, it becomes cooled. All air contains invisible water vapour, but if the air is cooled it can't hold as much vapour. So some of the water vapour turns into water droplets, which makes the fog over the water.

What's permafrost and how far north is it?

It's ground that's always frozen. It's **perma**nently **frost**y. The top layer might thaw during the summer, but the ground underneath will still be frozen. Permafrost covers much of Canada's North. On some Arctic islands the permafrost layer is up to 700 metres (3,000 ft.) thick! As you travel farther south, less and less of the ground is permanently frozen. The only permafrost found in the south is in the high mountains.

Is it possible to see an upside-down rainbow? My dad says he's seen one.

Are you sure your dad wasn't standing on his head? If not, maybe what he saw wasn't a rainbow but another colourful thing in the sky called—ready for this?—a circumzenithal arc. It's caused by light shining through ice crystals of a certain shape, and it looks like an upside-down rainbow.

WHAT MAKES A RAINBOW?

The sun has to shine from behind you through water droplets in the air ahead of you. The drops act like prisms, bending the light and separating it into the seven colours you see. A good time to look for rainbows is right after a rain shower when there are lots of large water droplets in the air. Make your own rainbow by standing with the sun at your back and spraying a fine mist of water from a garden hose in front of you. (Don't "accidentally" spray your little sister.)

Ask me something cold! I'm ready for it!

Hot, or Not!

Why is it so cold up north?

In the tropics, the sun shines straight down on the Earth, providing maximum heat. But in the Far North, the sun is low in the sky and the sun's rays come in at an angle. They don't warm things up very much. (Then of course, in winter, there are days when the sun doesn't rise above the horizon at all.) As well, the snow and ice *reflect* sunlight instead of absorbing it. Until the snow and ice have melted, which may not be until the middle of summer, the ground won't start to get warm. So in spite of almost 24-hour summer sunshine, temperatures rise above freezing for only a few weeks a year. Even then, just a metre below the surface, the ground is permanently frozen.

Who says it's cold?

Ptarmigan in an Arctic landscape.

Where's the hottest place in Canada?

Who says it's hot?

Tied for first place, with the highest average summer temperatures, are the interior valleys of British Columbia (near towns like Lytton and Kelowna) and the extreme southwest of Ontario. However, the highest temperature ever recorded was somewhere else—at Midvale and Yellow Grass, Saskatchewan. On July 5, 1937, the thermometer there reached 45°C (113°F).

West coast   East coast

Why does Vancouver get rain while Halifax gets so much snow?

Both Vancouver and Halifax are affected by oceans. The ocean is like a huge bathtub that takes a long time to heat up or cool down. It keeps both Vancouver and Halifax from getting too hot in summer or too cold in winter. But Vancouver's winter is warmer than Halifax's because of those warm, soggy Pacific storms that dump a lot of rain and mean warmer air coming off the Pacific Ocean. Meanwhile, the nearby mountain ranges block cold inland air from reaching Vancouver. So the average January temperature is a balmy 4°C (39°F). At the other end of the country, Nova Scotia gets two kinds of weather—storms from the Atlantic Ocean and cold air blowing in from central Canada. Halifax gets some spectacular blizzards and ice storms. The average January temperature is about -4°C (25°F). That explains the snow.

What caused the Great Dust Bowl in the 1930s?

The long drought (= no rain) that took place in the 1930s turned the Prairies into a dust bowl. The soil became so dry and dusty that the wind blew it away in huge dust storms. Many farmers went broke. Drought is just something that happens from time to time on the Prairies. Every thirty years or so there's a dry spell. Today, farmers leave a layer of stubble (what's left of the plants after the crop has been harvested) in the ground to keep the soil in place. The Prairies are now less dusty. But unless we figure out how to make rain when we need it, droughts will continue to plague Prairie farmers.

A southern Alberta farm in the 1930s.

Morton, tell me that bit about
how to lasso an iceberg again?

Get a Grip on Icebergs

How big do icebergs get?

The largest iceberg ever recorded in Canadian waters (in 1882 near Baffin Island) was 13 kilometres (8 mi.) long and 6 kilometres (3 3/4 mi.) wide, weighing more than 9 billion tonnes. That's pretty impressive! But it's a mere ice cube compared to some of the icebergs from Antarctica. In 2001, iceberg B-15A broke off from Antarctica's ice shelf. It was 295 kilometres (183 mi.) long and 38 kilometres (24 mi.) wide—twice the size of Prince Edward Island!

What are icebergs really made of?

Icebergs are made of glacial freshwater, not saltwater. It's so pure and unpolluted that stores in Newfoundland sell harvested iceberg water. People have even thought about towing icebergs to desert countries where drinking water is scarce—but they'd melt before they got there.

How far south can an iceberg travel before it melts?

In 1926, an iceberg was sighted as far south as Bermuda! But most icebergs stay closer to home in cold, Arctic waters. Most of our icebergs come from Greenland, the huge island north of Canada. A small number escape and are carried south by the Labrador current. Iceberg Alley (where the *Titanic* struck an iceberg in 1912) is the route bergs take as they drift south along the eastern coast of Newfoundland down to the Grand Bank. Once the bergs meet the warmer waters of the Gulf Stream current, you can guess what happens. Within a few months the once mighty icebergs are no more.

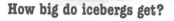

Labrador

Newfoundland

Nova Scotia

Iceberg Alley

Why do icebergs float all over the place?

They float because there's air trapped inside the ice. Only one-eighth of the iceberg shows above water, though. Most of it is underwater, so the berg goes where the ocean currents take it.

MORTON'S IRRESISTIBLE DETOUR

How do you stop a 10-million-tonne iceberg from ploughing through an offshore oil drilling platform? You lasso it! A ship dragging a floating tow line circles the iceberg. The ends of the tow line are joined together. Then VERY carefully (you don't want it to tip over), the iceberg is towed away from its chosen path.

Interview with Dr. Stephen Bruneau, a.k.a. Dr. Iceberg.

Vivien: Why are you so crazy about icebergs?

Dr. Bruneau: Because I grew up in Newfoundland and Labrador. When I was a kid my dad took part in the first experiments with towing icebergs. Later, I became involved in towing icebergs towards cliffs and crashing them into steel structures to test the force of impact. Fun stuff.

Vivien: Ouch! Why were you so mean to icebergs?

Dr. Bruneau: Icebergs are a danger to offshore oil drilling platforms. So engineers look for ways the platforms can be designed to withstand 5-million-tonne iceberg impacts.

Vivien: What else have you done to icebergs?

Dr. Bruneau: We tried blowing them up to make them smaller. Because icebergs are mostly underwater, the huge ones scrape along the shallow ocean floor. That's a problem for underwater pipelines. So we demolished really huge bergs with explosives, turning them into smaller bergs that floated off the bottom.

Dr. Stephen Bruneau

51

How do we get down?

Good question!

Tree Talk

Can forest fires burn all year even under the snow?

The answer to your burning question is yes. A fire may burn into tree roots underground. There, it smolders throughout the winter under an insulating layer of dirt and snow. It burns slowly because it gets very little oxygen. In the spring, when the snow melts and the ground dries out, the fire may burst into flames at the surface. To put it out properly, firefighters may have to dig it up first.

Why are there no trees in the Far North?

As you travel north, the trees grow smaller and smaller, until eventually they don't grow at all. The problem is not that they can't survive the cold. It's that they need warm summers for growing. Even though the Arctic summer has days with almost 24 hours of sunlight, the amount of time when it's actually warm enough for plants to grow is very short. During that short period, Arctic plants put all their energy into growing the essentials: roots and leaves (not trunks).

Where are the largest maple leaves?

On a big-leaf maple tree, be*leaf* it or not. Big-leaf maples have leaves that are more than 30 centimetres (12 in.) across—bigger than this page. They grow along the British Columbia coast.

Where is Canada's tallest tree?

Canada's tallest tree is the Carmanah Giant, a 95 metre (310 ft.) tall Sitka spruce tree growing on the west coast of Vancouver Island, British Columbia. It's taller than the Peace Tower in Ottawa (that's the tall tower on the Parliament Buildings).

Why do leaves change colours in the fall?

Leaves don't really change colours. They just lose their green, revealing the yellow and orange that have been there all along. When the days grow shorter and colder, the leaves stop producing the chemical called chlorophyll, and the green gradually disappears. Hello yellow and orange fall leaves. Red leaves are different. Sap is trapped in the leaves of the trees, and sunlight makes the sap turn bright red or purple.

How do trees grow so big?

Trees have sturdy wood trunks that hold them up and allow them to grow tall. Imagine if a dandelion tried to grow as tall as a tree—its stem would break. Also, trees keep adding to their growth each year. Since trees are the oldest living things on Earth, they have had plenty of growing time.

We're digging for answers, Morton.

Ear to the Ground

Why do the best potatoes grow on P.E.I.?

Nice spuds!

It's because of Prince Edward Island's famous red soil. The rich soil is light, sandy, free of stones, and easy to dig. P.E.I.'s long, cold winters freeze deep into the soil, killing any nasties that might cause potato diseases. Also, the island is separated from the mainland by water, which further protects it from potato diseases found elsewhere.

Potato field

How does the Magnetic Hill in New Brunswick work?

Magnetic Hill, near Moncton, is where cars roll uphill. At least, that's what it looks like. Drivers sit in their cars at the bottom of the gentle hill, and watch dumbfounded as they coast to the top. But it's really an optical illusion. At Magnetic Hill, the uphill is actually slightly downhill. Usually we know what's uphill and what's downhill by comparing it to the flat horizon. But around Magnetic Hill, the land is hilly so you can't see the horizon well. Also, the trees, which usually show us which way is straight up, grow slanted at Magnetic Hill. Our brains get fooled.

Why are there so few farms in Newfoundland?

Number one: poor soil for farming. Newfoundland is nicknamed "The Rock" for good reason. Number two: poor climate for growing crops. The growing season is short, and there is not much sunshine.

How did the Athabasca Sand Dunes get there?

The Athabasca Sand Dunes in northern Saskatchewan make up Canada's greatest sandbox! A billion years ago, an ancient river flowed into an ancient lake and dumped a load of sand and silt. Over the years, it hardened into a rock called sandstone. Over more years, wind and weather worked on the sandstone and ground it back into sand. These dunes are active! When the wind blows the sand around, the dunes move. Sometimes they uncover dead trees that have been buried for hundreds of years.

Are there deserts in Canada?

Real deserts? Well, no. A true desert is supposed to be hot and dry, with less than 25 centimetres (10 in.) of rain in a year. We have some very desert-like places in southern Canada where you can see the same kind of plants and animals you'd find in a desert. One is the so-called "pocket desert" in the southern Okanagan area of British Columbia. The Arctic is sometimes called a polar desert because it gets less than 15 centimetres (6 in.) of precipitation per year.

Get Wet

Niagara Falls

Where does all the water come from that goes over Niagara Falls?

Let's go right to the source.

Let's start at Niagara Falls, then head up the Niagara River to Lake Erie. That's where the water comes from. But where does Lake Erie's water come from, you ask. Well, most of it comes down the Detroit River from Lake Huron. And where does Lake Huron's water come from? Most of that water flows in from Lake Michigan, because Lake Huron and Lake Michigan are really one big lake, as well as from Lake Superior. So the water that ends up flowing over Niagara Falls comes from four Great Lakes: Superior, Michigan, Huron, and Erie. That's a huge amount of the world's fresh water!

Why does the Red River flood so much?

Flood coming. Man the lifeboats!

In spring or early summer, the Red River rushes north into Manitoba from the United States, heading for Lake Winnipeg. It carries water from all the melting snow that has poured into the river during its 630 kilometre (390 mi.) trip north. Some years there's more snow, and it all melts at once. The rushing river overflows its banks, and the province turns into a big puddle. The Red River floods so often they've built a big canal around Winnipeg so some of the water can bypass the city.

Flooding from the Red River.

HEAD-SCRATCHER

Why is water wet?

A mind-boggling question that tied my eyebrows into knots! Okay, here goes. Water, like everything else, is made of molecules. They are way too small to see. Water makes your hands wet because these water molecules stick to each other and to the surface of your skin. Each water molecule acts like a tiny magnet. Just as two magnets pull towards each other, water molecules and the surface of your skin attract one another. That's what makes your hands wet— water molecules are stuck on. Water also sticks to the cover of your social studies book when you leave it out in the rain. But water doesn't stick to everything. It rolls off waterproof raincoats and freshly waxed cars. The molecules on those surfaces aren't attracted to water molecules. So they don't get wet.

What's the white stuff in the lake that looks like snow?

That's shoreline foam, and it is natural and harmless. When plants and animals in the lake rot and become gucky, that stuff gets churned up by wind and waves, mixes with air, and becomes foam. Like a milkshake. (I did NOT say to drink it!)

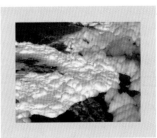

We're not talking about ice hockey (yet), Morton.

Cold Truths and Frozen Facts

How much of Canada is covered by ice?

About 200,000 square kilometres (77,226 sq. mi.), or about 2%, of the country is covered by glaciers and icefields year round. These icefields are found in the mountains out west and in the eastern Arctic. They are left over from the last ice age 15,000 years ago, when most of the country was in a deep freeze. But Canada's glaciers are shrinking, or "retreating." The climate is getting warmer, which means that more ice is melting from the "toe" of the glacier each year than is replaced by new snow falling on top.

Ever wonder what the glaciers have been hiding? As the world's glaciers retreat, they are revealing things that were covered by the ice. Archaeologists (scientists who study artifacts from long ago) have found tools, hunting weapons, and even human bodies that have been frozen for thousands of years. Most people are sad to see the glaciers melting, but archaeologists can't wait to see what the glacier will cough up next!

Alright, glacier, start talking. What have you been hiding in there?

Athabasca Glacier, Jasper National Park

Why is the ice that hangs off mountainsides blue?

Usually ice has air bubbles in it that reflect the light, making the ice look white. But the ice in a glacier (which is what hangs off a mountain, often in the form of an icefall) is made of snow that has most of the air squashed out of it. So instead of being reflected, light penetrates deep into the ice, where most of it is absorbed. Only the blue light bounces back, so that's what you see. It gives the glacier its deep, turquoise colour.

Why are some lakes in the Rockies a distinctive colour?

The water that flows into those mountain lakes comes from melting glaciers. This meltwater contains a chalk-like powder called glacial silt, or rock flour. This silt is so fine it doesn't fall to the bottom of the lake, but instead is suspended in the water. The silt absorbs all the colours of incoming light except for the blue-green colour we see when we look at the lake.

Peyto Lake, Alberta

This is firsthand quicksand research.

Rock 'n' Dirt

Is there any quicksand in Canada?

I have a sinking feeling about this.

Yes indeed. Quicksand is found along beaches, marshes, lakes, and riverbanks. But it isn't the scary stuff shown in the movies. It won't suck you down into a bottomless pit, never to be heard from again. It's just ordinary sand mixed with so much water it becomes soupy and can't hold your weight. So you sink—but usually not farther than your knees. Struggling or thrashing around makes you sink more. Just relax and make slow movements. Your body can actually float on the surface of quicksand. No need to panic.

How did hoodoos form?

Hoodoos are nature's amazing sculptures. The rock towers look like huge mushrooms. Water and wind sculpt away the soft sandstone rock underneath, leaving the harder layer of rock (the mushroom cap) on top. Southern Alberta is a good place to hide among hoodoos.

Hoodoos in Drumheller, Alberta

Why is Prince Edward Island's dirt so red?

It's from iron in the soil. When iron gets wet, it rusts and turns red.

How was the Canadian Shield made?

It was a major, very time-consuming landscaping project. Long ago, where the Canadian Shield is now was an ancient, volcanic landscape with mountain ranges as high as today's Rockies. That landscape was left out in wind, rain, and snow for a couple of billion years until it was worn down. Glaciers covering Canada during the ice ages did further damage, scraping away the softer earth, removing the top dirt layer and exposing the older "basement rock" underneath. The result is today's Canadian Shield, a generally flat and rocky landscape dotted with lakes and puddles. It forms an enormous U-shape surrounding Hudson Bay and covering about half of Canada. It's where some of the oldest rocks on Earth are exposed—they're 3.6 billion years old. Much of the Shield is covered by forests that stretch north to the treeline.

What gems or semi-precious stones are found in Canada?

We'll go rockhounding! Grab your rock hammer and safety goggles. First a quick scoop of diamonds from the Northwest Territories. Then it's off to Labrador to find labradorite. (Gee, I wonder how it got its name.) Now, to the world-renowned "Magic Mountain," also known as Mount St. Hilaire, Quebec. There we'll look for rare and unusual gems such as rhodochrosite, hilairite, serandite, lukechangite, and gobbinsite. A couple of stops in Ontario: first to the Bancroft area for blue-coloured sodalite and rose quartz, then to the Thunder Bay area for amethysts. In southern Alberta we'll find ammolite, which comes from the shells of long-dead, 200-million-year-old sea snails called ammonites. In northern British Columbia and the Yukon we might get lucky and find rubies, sapphires, and emeralds—geologists figure there are lots there. Then we'll get some green jade from British Columbia, and a garnet or two.

Rhodochrosite

Whoa—my backpack is getting heavy!

Okay, we've hounded enough rocks for today.

Sodalite

Amethyst

I can't see a thing down here!   Turn on your headlamp, Morton!

Going Underground

What's the deepest mine in Canada?

The Creighton nickel-copper mine in Sudbury, Ontario, is the deepest, and it's still going down. The mine is already more than 2,300 metres (7,545 ft.) deep, but in 20 years that will increase to over 2,460 metres (8,070 ft.)—deep enough to bury Toronto's CN Tower four and a half times.

Why would anyone want to bury the CN Tower?

I've no idea. It sure would ruin the view.

Creighton mine, Sudbury, Ontario

How do we know we're not blowing up dinosaur bones when we blast the Earth?

"Dinosaurish" is not in my cyber dictionary.

A regrettable omission.

We can't know for sure. But in Alberta, the most dinosaurish part of Canada, mining companies planning to blow up rock must first hire a palaeontologist to check for the possibility of fossils. They decide if the rock is the kind that might contain fossils. Then they'll check the ground for any little bits of bone. If they find anything, they'll dig further to investigate. Dinosaur fossils are very rare, however. And sometimes mining actually helps palaeontologists make exciting discoveries. At a mine in western Alberta, thousands of dinosaur footprints have been discovered underneath a layer of coal. Without the mining, these prints may have never been found.

One diamond mine in the Northwest Territories produces 8 million carats a year!

Did someone say carrots?

SIRIUS 🐻 A2-031Z

Not carrots, carats. That's how you measure the size of diamonds.

Where are the diamond mines in Canada?

Go north! Canada's first diamond mine was in the Northwest Territories, about 300 kilometres (185 mi.) northeast of Yellowknife, practically in the middle of nowhere. The geologist who found the diamond deposit had been hunting for ten years. Now he's rich. In addition to the N.W.T., both Nunavut and northern Ontario are starting up diamond mines. Canada is the world's third-largest producer of diamonds. All of our diamonds are etched with a teensy polar bear (see above).

MORTON'S IRRESISTIBLE DETOUR

Diamonds are formed more than 150 kilometres (95 mi.) deep underground. That's rather inconvenient. Fortunately, they are carried to the surface by volcanic activity. Magma, red-hot liquified rock, under pressure, explodes up to the surface. It cools and hardens into an ice cream cone-shaped rock formation called a kimberlite pipe. Years later, geologists look for kimberlite pipes, because they know that's where the diamonds are hiding. Oops, there's one catch. Kimberlite pipes usually have lakes on top of them. These lakes need to be drained before you can dig for diamonds.

How far underground are we going this time?

Over two kilometres down. We'd better pack a lunch.

Deep Questions

What on Earth are neutrinos?

It's pronounced "New tree no."

Neutrinos are smaller than you can imagine. You may have heard of atoms, which are certainly small. Well, neutrinos are much, much smaller. These teensy particles are thrown out from the sun and come zinging to Earth. The sun produces over two hundred trillion trillion trillion neutrinos every second. You can't see them or feel them. They're so tiny they can pass right through you and out the other side—billions of them each second. Eeeek! (Finding it hard to imagine something going *through* you? Think of X-rays that go through your body and allow doctors and dentists to see the bones inside.)

How do scientists capture neutrinos?

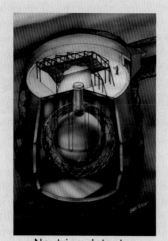

Neutrino detector

Physicists study neutrinos to learn more about how the sun burns. Since the sun is just one of many stars, neutrinos also provide clues to understanding how the entire universe evolved. But how can you study something so tiny? Well, you need a neutrino detector.

Neutrino detectors don't come small or cheap. Canada, with help from the United States and Great Britain, has built a huge one called the Sudbury Neutrino Observatory (nicknamed SNO). It's in a mine over 2 kilometres (1.2 mi.) underground near Sudbury, Ontario. The rock above filters out other rays that hit the Earth's surface from all over the universe and might get in the way of detecting neutrinos. Imagine being inside a huge cavern the size of a ten-storey building excavated from the rock. The walls are lined with plastic because the detector needs to be kept super-clean. Inside this cavern is a huge, transparent plastic sphere 12 metres (39 ft.) in diameter, suspended by ropes. Inside the sphere is 1,000 tonnes of "heavy water" (it contains molecules that are a bit different and heavier than those in regular water). This heavy water itself costs over $300 million. Surrounding the sphere is a geodesic dome on which are mounted 9,600 light sensors.

The neutrino trap is now set. Most neutrinos from the sun pass straight through the Earth and through the heavy water without being detected. But a very few, maybe one each hour, happen to hit the water in precisely the right way so that they are stopped. Gotcha!

Canada's underground neutrino detector, Creighton mine, Sudbury, Ontario

This land is your land... This land is my land...

Far and Wide

Alaska Highway

What is the farthest north that we can travel by car in Canada? Who would we meet there?

Did somebody just say "muskox stew?"

Hop in. We're driving up the Alaska Highway. From Dawson Creek in British Columbia, we'll drive towards Dawson City in the Yukon. Just before Dawson City we'll turn onto the Dempster Highway and continue north over 741 kilometres (460 mi.) of gravel road, crossing over the Arctic Circle, entering the Northwest Territories, and ending up in Inuvik. We can get out now. We've gone as far as we can go. Dip your big toe into the Mackenzie River. Wait—if we stay here until the ground freezes in winter, we can go even farther. There's an ice road that will take us another 137 kilometres (85 mi.) to Tuktoyaktuk, on the Arctic Ocean. That's where we'll get out.

Who will we meet in Tuk? Most of the people living there are Inuvialuit (that's what the Inuit living there call themselves). Perhaps we'll meet an oil rig worker drilling in the Beaufort Sea. Or someone who will take us ice fishing, and invite us in for muskox stew.

This beaver tail is made of pastry. They call it a "beaver tail" just for fun.

Strange sense of humour.

How long would it take to walk from one side of Canada to the other while stopping for one beaver tail in Ottawa?

Let's say you'll walk 5 kilometres (3 mi.) per hour for five hours each day—that's 25 kilometres (15 1/2 mi.) per day. And it's 6,119 kilometres (3,802 mi.) along the highway from Halifax, Nova Scotia, to Vancouver, British Columbia. So it would take you (...I know, it's long division, but do it anyway...) 244.76 days. So just under 245 days. Don't forget to stop for a beaver tail. That will add about 10 minutes to your time.

...this land was made for you and me.

Choo-Choo Bear and the Polar Bear Express Train

How far north do trains go?

I found a train that goes even farther north! The Great Slave Lake Railway runs north from Alberta to Hay River, Northwest Territories, carrying supplies to northern mines and communities.

All aboard! In Ontario, you can take the Polar Bear Express train north to Moose Factory, on the shores of James Bay. Better yet, in Manitoba, you can hop on the train to Churchill, on the shores of Hudson Bay. That's farther north. Wait, this is even better! On the Pacific coast, the White Pass & Yukon Route Railroad starts at Skagway, Alaska, chugs up mountainsides and across the U.S.–Canada border, and ends up in Bennett, British Columbia, almost at the Yukon border.

Are there any roads leading to Nunavut?

No roads. You have to fly there. But when you arrive in some Nunavut communities such as Iqaluit or Cambridge Bay, you'll find that there are roads around town. Some residents bring in vehicles by ship. In Iqaluit, you'll even see school buses. But most people find that ATVs (All Terrain Vehicles) or snowmobiles are a better way to get around.

Borderlines

Who decided how to divide up the provinces and territories?

The truth is, most of it wasn't very well planned. That's why some provinces are huge while others are tiny. Provinces and territories were added to Canada at various times in history. Often there were arguments over where the borders should go.

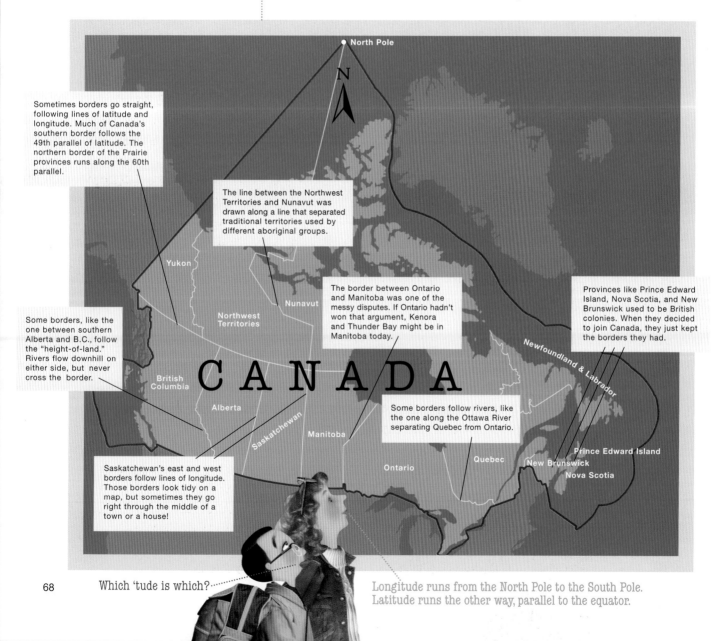

North Pole

Sometimes borders go straight, following lines of latitude and longitude. Much of Canada's southern border follows the 49th parallel of latitude. The northern border of the Prairie provinces runs along the 60th parallel.

The line between the Northwest Territories and Nunavut was drawn along a line that separated traditional territories used by different aboriginal groups.

The border between Ontario and Manitoba was one of the messy disputes. If Ontario hadn't won that argument, Kenora and Thunder Bay might be in Manitoba today.

Provinces like Prince Edward Island, Nova Scotia, and New Brunswick used to be British colonies. When they decided to join Canada, they just kept the borders they had.

Some borders, like the one between southern Alberta and B.C., follow the "height-of-land." Rivers flow downhill on either side, but never cross the border.

Some borders follow rivers, like the one along the Ottawa River separating Quebec from Ontario.

Saskatchewan's east and west borders follow lines of longitude. Those borders look tidy on a map, but sometimes they go right through the middle of a town or a house!

Yukon

Nunavut

Northwest Territories

British Columbia

Alberta

Saskatchewan

Manitoba

Ontario

Quebec

Newfoundland & Labrador

New Brunswick

Prince Edward Island

Nova Scotia

CANADA

68

Which 'tude is which?

Longitude runs from the North Pole to the South Pole. Latitude runs the other way, parallel to the equator.

MORTON'S IRRESISTIBLE DETOUR

The Canada–U.S. border goes through the middle of several buildings. For instance, it goes through an opera house in Rock Island, Quebec. The stage is in Canada, but the audience's seats are in the United States.

Haskell Opera House in Quebec and Vermont

How did people decide where to draw the border between Canada and the United States?

Canada—U.S. border crossing

It took many years, many squabbles, a few wars, and lots of negotiating. There were treaties, International Boundary Commissions, and lots of official documents sealed with wax and tied with red ribbon.

A good place to start is with the Treaty of Paris in 1783. Before that, the United States didn't exist. It was created after 13 British colonies, who didn't want to be British anymore, started the American Revolution. The Treaty of Paris ended the big fight and set the border between the newly independent United States and the part of North America that remained British (what's now southern Ontario and Quebec).

In the west, the 49th parallel became the border from Lake of the Woods in Ontario all the way to the Pacific Ocean. But the president of the United States in 1844 didn't agree. He wanted the border west of the Rockies to be farther north. Meanwhile, Great Britain wanted the boundary farther south, along the Columbia River. This big fight was called the Oregon Boundary Dispute, which sounds much more polite than it really was. The dispute was settled by the Oregon Treaty in 1846, which put the boundary where it is today, along the 49th parallel.

Why isn't Alaska part of Canada?

History is a story that could have had many different endings. Think how Canada would look today if it didn't include the Canadian Shield. Or, what if British Columbia, which joined Canada in 1871, had instead joined the United States, a popular idea at the time?

Because the United States bought it first. Alaska belonged to Russia before 1867 (the Russians had arrived there first, looking for furs), when the Americans bought it from the Russians for 7.2 million dollars. Some Americans thought their government was nuts to spend all that cash for a frozen chunk of land they nicknamed "Icebergia." Both America and Canada (which at the time was much smaller, only a few eastern provinces) wanted to expand. Shortly after America obtained Alaska, Canada bought a vast area of land from the Hudson's Bay Company, Rupert's Land, which included the Canadian Shield. Suddenly Canada was bigger than the United States, so there!

Wow, look at these headlines. Some of this stuff is unbelievable!

That's why I'm wearing my Critical Thinking Cap, Morton. It reminds me to question information I find, especially on the Web. Anybody can post on the Web, so I ask myself: Is it true? Who wrote it? Are they well informed? Here, I'll lend you my CT Cap.

No! I mean...I don't think I actually need to wear a hat. Not a real one, anyway. I'll just wear a sort of virtual CT Cap.

Morton, I'm beginning to think you don't like my beautiful CT Cap.

Oh, look at that, I have incoming e-mail. I'm due at chess club in 17 minutes. Gotta go!

Critical Thinking Cap

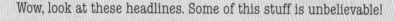
Finder   File   Edit   View   Go   Window   Help   Tue 10.28

UFO Lands on Toronto's CN Tower

3-Headed Moose Gives Birth to Chipmunks!

Beaver Observed Singing "O Canada"—in Both Official Languages!

Does the original Canadian flag still exist?

How do you build an igloo?

These questions are about things that Canadians do or have done. How we live, the languages we speak, our history, and our "Canadian" habits.

CHAPTER 3

Explain Yourselves, Canadians!

Who's Bruce?

BRUCE TRAIL

Why Name It *That?*

Why is Canada called "Canada?"

So many of you asked that! The name "Canada" started as a mistake. When French explorer Jacques Cartier was exploring up the St. Lawrence River in 1535, the two aboriginal guides on board his ship pointed out their village (situated at the site of today's Quebec City). "Kanata," they said, which in their Huron-Iroquois language meant "village" or "settlement." But Cartier thought they were telling him the name of the village, so he started calling it Kanata or Canada (although the village was actually called Stadacona). The big river running by the village (which is now called the St. Lawrence River) became the "rivière de Canada." Soon all the land around the river started being called "Canada," too. As explorers went exploring and found more land, "Canada" grew and grew. For a time in the early 1700s, it even included lots of what's now in the United States. Later there was an Upper Canada, a Lower Canada, and a Province of Canada. Finally in 1867, when this country was officially formed, it was named Canada!

CANADA

The Bruce Trail in Ontario is named for the Bruce Peninsula, but WHO IS BRUCE?

This was a very tricky search—but I did finally manage to track down Bruce! His name was James Bruce, the 8th Earl of Elgin. (He's usually listed under "Lord Elgin" instead of "Bruce," which is why I couldn't find him.) Bruce was the governor general of the province of Canada in 1847, back when Canada was still a British colony. He helped Canada establish responsible government, where decisions are made by elected representatives. Before that, only a few powerful people were making all the decisions, which wasn't fair. Three cheers for Bruce! By the time Bruce County was named after him, in 1867, James Bruce, a.k.a. Lord Elgin, had been sent to India to be its governor, and had died there.

BRUCE TRAIL

I thought Bruce was his first name!

What is the weirdest Canadian place name?

Here are some contenders. Which one do you think is the weirdest?

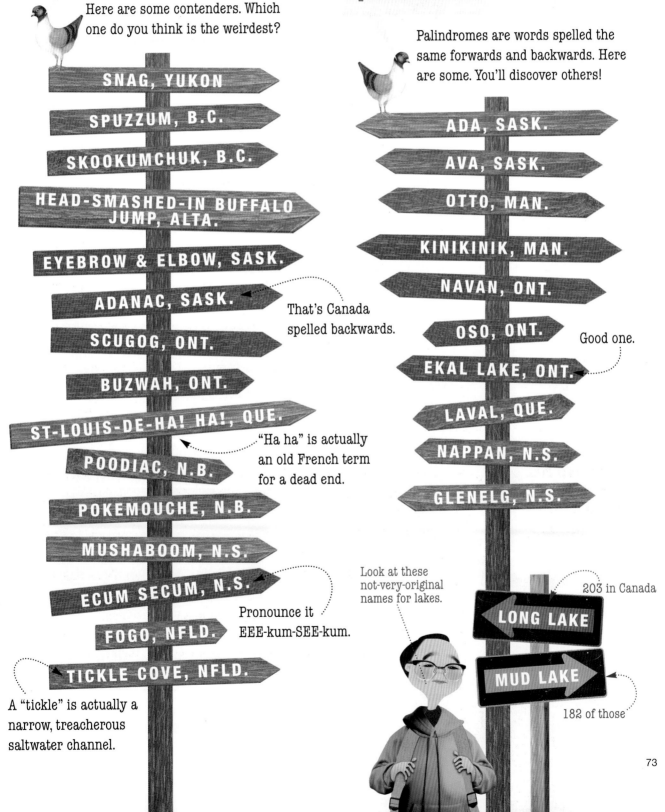

SNAG, YUKON

SPUZZUM, B.C.

SKOOKUMCHUK, B.C.

HEAD-SMASHED-IN BUFFALO JUMP, ALTA.

EYEBROW & ELBOW, SASK.

ADANAC, SASK.

That's Canada spelled backwards.

SCUGOG, ONT.

BUZWAH, ONT.

ST-LOUIS-DE-HA! HA!, QUE.

"Ha ha" is actually an old French term for a dead end.

POODIAC, N.B.

POKEMOUCHE, N.B.

MUSHABOOM, N.S.

ECUM SECUM, N.S.

Pronounce it EEE-kum-SEE-kum.

FOGO, NFLD.

TICKLE COVE, NFLD.

A "tickle" is actually a narrow, treacherous saltwater channel.

How many place names, like Wakaw, Saskatchewan, are palindromes?

Palindromes are words spelled the same forwards and backwards. Here are some. You'll discover others!

ADA, SASK.

AVA, SASK.

OTTO, MAN.

KINIKINIK, MAN.

NAVAN, ONT.

OSO, ONT.

EKAL LAKE, ONT.

Good one.

LAVAL, QUE.

NAPPAN, N.S.

GLENELG, N.S.

Look at these not-very-original names for lakes.

203 in Canada

← LONG LAKE

MUD LAKE →

182 of those

73

Make sure you get the proportions right.

Your nose is in the way.

Raise the Flag!

Why does the Canadian flag look the way it does?

How did we come up with our flag? We formed a committee! The committee received thousands of suggestions—flags with both French and English symbols, with beavers chomping down trees, and one with three green maple leaves between two blue borders. The committee settled on a single red maple leaf. The final design was a group effort: one person decided the shape of the leaf, another the proportions of red and white, and another the shade of red that would look best.

Members of Parliament argued over the flag. There was debating, shouting, pontificating, cheering, pounding on desks, getting red in the face, and flag-waving. Finally, at 2:15 in the morning on December 15, 1964, parliament voted to accept this new Canadian flag.

Why does Canada's flag have a maple leaf and why is it red?

Ruby?
Scarlet?
Blood red?
Crimson?
Tomato red?
Fire engine red?
Vermillion?
FIP red No. 509-211?

Maple leaves have been a Canadian symbol for almost two hundred years. In 1867, a song called "The Maple Leaf For Ever" was written to celebrate the occasion of Canada becoming a country. Maple leaves began sprouting on official coats of arms and on coins. Canada's Olympic athletes wore a red maple leaf on a white background in 1904.

Why red? Red and white were proclaimed Canada's official colours by the King of England in 1921. The tricky part was deciding exactly what shade of red to use. They decided that if you're painting a Canadian flag, you should use FIP red No. 509-211. Now you know.

MORTON'S IRRESISTIBLE DETOUR

Here's how to tell if you have an old Canadian maple leaf flag—the red will have turned orange! The first batch of flags, raised across the country and around the world in 1965, used a red dye that became orange-coloured over time. Afterwards, the government put its scientists to work to come up with a red dye for the flag that would *stay* red.

I think I have an idea for a better design.

WE'RE NOT CHANGING IT!

I love this new flag!

Such a flap over a flag!

What year did the Canadian flag start being used?

Bong! Bong! At exactly noon on February 15, 1965, the old Canadian flag, the Red Ensign, was lowered and, for the first time, the maple leaf flag was raised on Parliament Hill. Thousands watched as the band played "O Canada." Similar ceremonies took place at noon in time zones across the country. The prime minister, Lester B. Pearson, had been trying to get a new flag for a long time. He was probably thrilled to finally see that red maple leaf flying in the sky above Canada.

Does the original Canadian flag still exist? Where is it kept?

I'm always finding stuff in the back of my closet.

There are two Canadian flags that might be considered the "original." One is the flag Joan O'Malley sewed in 1964. Joan's father, who worked for the government of Canada, had to come up with samples of three of the proposed Canadian flags—which at that time were only designs on paper—for Prime Minister Pearson.

It was Friday night, and Pearson wanted the flags for the weekend. Joan's father needed someone to make them. Fast! His daughter agreed to do it. Joan didn't know then that one of the flags she was sewing would become Canada's official flag. That flag has since been destroyed.

The other "original" Canadian flag is the official one that was raised on Parliament Hill on February 15, 1965. For years it was lost. But in 2004, it was found—in Belgium! It had been given to the Speaker of the House of Commons (the one who had to keep order during all the arguments over the flag) shortly after the flag-raising ceremony. He kept it in a wooden box in his closet. He later moved to Belgium. After his death, his wife found the flag and returned it to Canada.

It's cold up here!

Welcome to the Arctic, Morton.

Up, Up, Up North!

No!

Do the Canadian Inuit really live in igloos?

They did a long time ago, but today they live in houses. Sometimes an Inuit who's out hunting or gets caught in a blizzard might build an igloo for an overnight shelter. But most Inuit live pretty much like Canadians farther south do, watching their favourite TV shows or eating macaroni and cheese for lunch.

Which Canadian school is closest to the North Pole? How many students go there?

For your information, *Umimmak* means muskox in Inuktitut.

Is Canada the only country with Inuit people?

How do you build an igloo?

Umimmak School, in Nunavut, is the most northerly school in Canada. It's in Grise Fiord, on Ellesmere Island, the Arctic island that's on the very "top" of Canada. There are 55 students, almost all Inuit. From kindergarten to grade 5, classes are taught in Inuktitut, the language of the Inuit. Students in grades 6 to 12 do most of their work in English.

Inuit also live in Greenland, Siberia (Russia), and Alaska (United States). They don't all use the name "Inuit," though. In Greenland, they call themselves *Kalaallit*. In Canada's western Arctic, they call themselves *Invialuit*.

Most Inuit are descendants of the *Thule* people, nomadic hunters who crossed the Bering Strait from Russia and spread across Arctic North America about 1,000 years ago. In Canada, most Inuit live in Nunavut. But there are also Inuit in Nunavik (northern Quebec), in Nunatsiavut (Labrador), and in the Northwest Territories—and in almost every Canadian province or territory.

Morton was all set to fly to the Arctic for this question. I convinced him to head for the computer instead.

1. We found a phone number for the Nunavut Department of Education by doing an Internet search using the words "Nunavut, education."
2. The woman who answered said she would e-mail a list of all the schools in Nunavut.
3. Morton and I put the list beside a map of Nunavut, and decided that Grise Fiord was farthest north. (The only community farther north, Alert, has no school.)
4. We sent an e-mail to the principal at the school in Grise Fiord. Here's what she told us.

How much longer until we can get inside and have some hot cocoa?

MORTON'S GUIDE TO BUILDING AN IGLOO

1. Find snow that's the right consistency to cut into blocks, so your blocks won't crumble. If there's no hard snow around, you can stomp on an area of snow, then let it freeze overnight.

2. Cut big blocks of snow with a knife, arranging them in a circle. Then add more layers of snow blocks. Lean them slightly inward so the walls come together and join at the top to form a sturdy dome.

3. Make an entrance.

4. Seal the cracks between the blocks with more snow. Smooth the inside walls. The heat from your seal oil lamp will warm the snow on the inside of the walls, then when it gets cold again it will freeze hard into ice and be incredibly strong.

健談的加拿大人。

Eh?

Oh, she's saying "Canadians have lots to say" in Cantonese.

Speak Up, Canada

Eh?

Eh?

Eh?

Eh?

I'm Canadian but I never say "eh?"

You don't, eh?

Why do some Canadians say "eh?"

We say "eh" because we're nice. It's a way of including the other person in the conversation. For instance, if we say, "Sure is hot, eh?" the "eh?" means, "Don't you think?" We don't just tell the person it's hot (which might sound bossy or opinionated). We check to see if that person agrees.

Or we might say, "I didn't have any money, eh? So I couldn't buy lunch." In this case the "eh?" is a way of checking that the other person understands.

Canadians aren't the only people to say, "eh," but we probably do it most often.

How many Teochiu-speaking people live in Canada? The only people I know that speak this language is my family.

Teochiu (some people call it Teochew or Chiu Chow) is a language originally from southeastern China. There are 20 million Teochiu-speakers worldwide. While most of them are in China and Southeast Asia, they've spread throughout the world, including to the United States and Canada. Nobody seems to keep accurate records, but there are about 200,000 to 300,000 Teochiu-speakers in Canada.

How many different languages are spoken in Canada?

English is the most common language spoken in Canada, followed by French. Then come Italian, German, Cantonese (Chinese), Punjabi, Spanish, Portugese, Polish, and Arabic. That's just for starters. Here's a bigger list of the more common languages spoken in Canada. Morton counted more than 100 languages on it before he gave up.

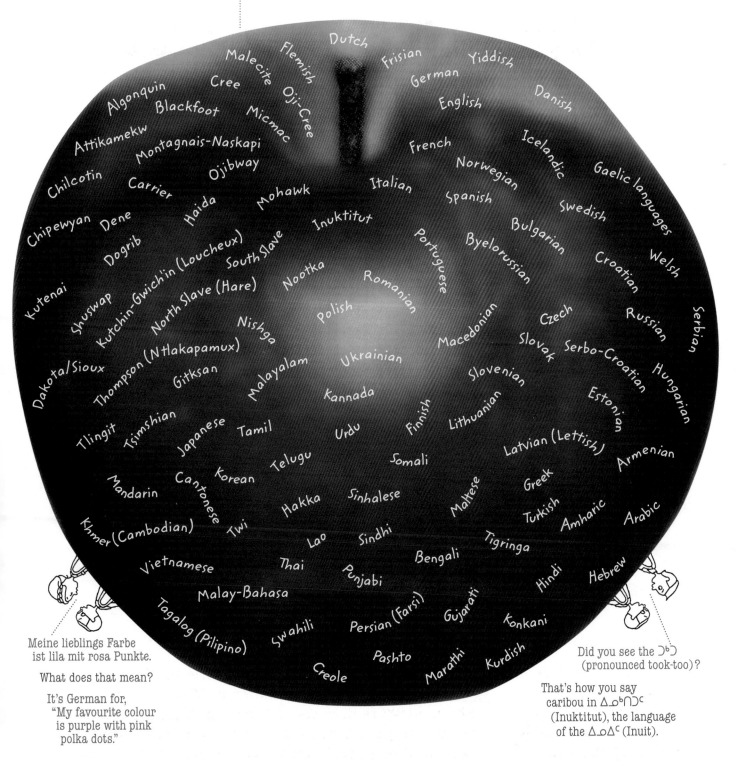

Meine lieblings Farbe
ist lila mit rosa Punkte.

What does that mean?

It's German for,
"My favourite colour
is purple with pink
polka dots."

Did you see the ᑐᒃᑑ
(pronounced took-too)?

That's how you say
caribou in ᐃᓄᒃᑎᑐᑦ
(Inuktitut), the language
of the ᐃᓄᐃᑦ (Inuit).

I can't look!

Hockey Hullabaloo

Why do Canadians love hockey sooo much?

We asked Roy MacGregor (see right) for help with this question, and this is what we came up with. Hockey is popular in Canada because:

 It's so c-c-c-cold in this country, we need a fast-moving game that gets the blood pumping. Hockey is exciting and action-packed! And we do have lots of handy frozen ponds.

It's *our* game. Canadians were the ones who started playing organized ice hockey in the late 1800s. We won the first-ever Olympic gold medal for hockey in 1924. Canadians are still the best on the ice…a lot of the time. That makes us feel good about the game and proud to be Canadian.

Hockey brings together grandparents and grandkids, French- and English-speakers, immigrants, Inuit, and those living in small towns and big cities.

"Hockey Night in Canada" has been broadcasting professional hockey games coast-to-coast for over 50 years on television, and even longer on radio. That's a lot of hockey hype, and it helps promote the game.

Isn't it time for the news?

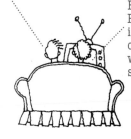

Forget the news. Right now the game is tied and we're in overtime. Looks like we might end in a shootout!

Why do Canadians love hockey? I know who to ask! Roy MacGregor—he wrote all those books about the Screech Owls, a fictional hockey team. He's a total hockey fan. I'll search for his Web page.

Dear Roy MacGregor:
This is Morton sending you an e-mail. Please explain: why is hockey soooooooooo popular in Canada? I look forward to your answer. Hopefully soon, because we're on a deadline.
Sincerely, Morton
(a Screech Owls fan)

Roy MacGregor

I love "Hockey Night in Canada!"

I can't get that theme music out of my head.

Ten million Canadians watched the Canadian men's hockey team win Olympic Gold in 2002.

I'm going to play in the NHL.

My favourite book is *The Hockey Sweater* by Roch Carrier.

Many Canadian babies are born with ice skates on their feet.

Hockey has become almost as much of a national symbol as the maple leaf or the beaver.

That might be a slight exaggeration.

That's former Prime Minister Lester Pearson talking hockey—in 1939!

First Nations: Now, Then and Way Back When

When and who was the first Beothuk Indian to land in Newfoundland?

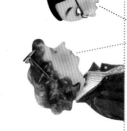

Did the Cow Head people have cow heads?

No, silly. They lived near a place that's now called "Cow Head."

The Beothuk were an aboriginal people living in Newfoundland when Europeans landed there. When the Beothuk themselves first arrived on the island is a mystery—there are no written records. But archaeologists are digging up evidence about Newfoundland's earliest residents.

They have decided that the Beothuk were probably descendants of the "Little Passage" people, who left behind razor-sharp arrowheads and scrapers made of greenish chert (a hard rock). And those Little Passage people were probably descendants of the "Beaches" people, who had used different rock for their tools. Those Beaches people might be descended from the even earlier "Cow Head" people. If the first Beothuk were Cow Head, that would mean they landed in Newfoundland at least 2,000 years ago.

Would a Cow Head person still be a Beothuk?

Sure. The same people were just called different names at different times. It's like Romans today are called Italians.

Don't quit backtracking yet! The Cow Head people may be descendants of people who lived in Newfoundland even earlier. Archaeologists call them the "Maritime Archaic" people. If that's the case, perhaps the first Beothuk arrived in Newfoundland 5,000 years ago! The further back you go, the more you're just guessing. The Beothuk people are all gone now—the last one, a young woman named Shanawdithit, died in 1829.

Is there anywhere in Canada where people still live in tipis?

You won't find many people living in tipis today. It's easier to plug in a microwave or install a washing machine in a house. Tipis are used more for ceremonial occasions, or to show people what they used to be like. Some people use tipis to go camping in the summer.

How many Native reserves are there in Canada? What is it like to live on one?

There are over 2,700 Native reserves across Canada. The people living on the reserves belong to any of the more than 600 different First Nations in Canada. For instance, they could be Tshimshian, Mi'kmaq, Dene, or Cree.

On a reserve, kids live in houses, go to school, and maybe play basketball or video games. Sound familiar? On many reserves, people also celebrate their aboriginal heritage. Cree kids on a reserve in Saskatchewan might learn traditional songs and dances. On the west coast, Haida high school students might make button blankets to wear at their graduation ceremonies. At the same time, First Nations kids are regular Canadian kids. They "forget" to do their homework and have to make their beds.

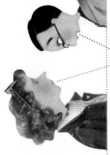

This isn't one of the questions, but I was wondering why we have reserves? That's allowed.

It's one of those historical things. When people from Europe settled across Canada in the 1800s, the First Nations got squeezed off their lands. So the Canadian government decided to put Native people on small areas called reserves. In return, the government said they would give them protection and some financial help. The First Nations didn't always understand that they were giving up their traditional lands in return for these reserves. Today, many aboriginal groups are negotiating new agreements with the government that recognize their traditional rights on these lands.

Have you looked down?

We're getting a new perspective on totem poles.

Tall Tales of Totem Poles

Where is the oldest totem pole in Canada?

Why are totem poles found only in British Columbia?
Can you guess why, Morton?
B.C. has lots of big trees. It would be hard finding a suitable tree for a totem pole, say, on the Prairies.
Very true.

It has probably returned to the forest floor. The thing about totem poles is that they don't last forever. They stand outside in the wind and rain, and in a hundred years or so they've fallen over and are covered with moss and ferns.

Canada's oldest totem poles are probably in the abandoned Haida village on Anthony Island (known as Sgang Gwaay by the Haida) on the southern tip of the Queen Charlotte Islands (Haida Gwaii). The village was abandoned in the 1880s, so the poles are at least that old.

Nobody knows how long the First Nations of the Northwest coast have been carving totem poles. Some poles existed when the first European explorers arrived on the coast over 200 years ago. But before that? There are no written records, and no really old poles still standing to tell the tale.

You shouldn't climb on totem poles, sit on them, or lean on them. That's being unrespectful.

I think you mean "disrespectful."

MORTON'S IRRESISTIBLE DETOUR

WHY YOU SHOULD NOT CLIMB TOTEM POLES

Totem poles show the history, legends, and traditions of a family or clan. They are like important family documents. The human and animal figures (called crests) have meanings, and together they tell a story. They might tell of long-ago journeys or heroic adventures, of marriages and births, of encounters with supernatural beings. Maybe you can find someone who can read the pole's story to you and explain what it means.

Why did collectors who visited the Queen Charlotte Islands take the totem poles?

In the past, hundreds of poles were removed from British Columbia coastal villages and put in museums and private collections in places such as Vancouver, Ottawa, New York, Paris, and Berlin.

People were fascinated by these huge sculptures and those who carved them. At the time, the collectors wanted to preserve some totem poles before they all disappeared. The culture of the Northwest Coast people was dying. Diseases such as smallpox had decimated the aboriginal population. Villages had been abandoned. Children had been taken from their families and sent to schools far from home where they weren't allowed to speak their language. The potlatch, an important ceremony held when a new totem pole was raised, was banned by the government. Many of the older totem pole carvers died without being able to pass on their knowledge to younger carvers.

Today we realize that the collectors should not have taken these totem poles and other cultural items without permission. And First Nations such as the Haida are taking a renewed interest in their traditional culture. They have begun insisting that museums return items that were taken from them more than a century ago. And look up—new totem poles are being carved and raised to the sky!

What does the expression "low man on the totem pole" mean?

It means someone is the least important person in a group. But that expression is actually upside-down, because on a totem pole, the "low man" at the bottom is generally the most important crest on the pole.

We'll paddle into history, Morton. Like the voyageurs!

Perhaps avoiding the rapids.

Historical Happenings

What was the most difficult portage the voyageurs had to endure as they crossed Canada by canoe?

It was hard enough to paddle canoes upstream with their heavy loads. But when the voyageurs had to haul everything over land between bodies of water on a portage, that was really back-breaking stuff. The voyageurs had to do the Methye portage to get over the height of land into the northern territories. On the south side, the rivers such as the mighty Churchill all flow east towards Hudson Bay. To get at the furs farther north and west, the traders needed to carry their goods over a ridge and down into the next drainage basin, where the rivers flow into the Mackenzie River and towards the Arctic Ocean.

Methye portage in northern Saskatchewan was the longest, toughest, sweatiest, and nastiest of all—a gruelling 19 kilometre (12 mi.) trail.

I have to be home by lunch. I might not have time for a portage today.

Why is the bay called Hudson Bay while the company is Hudson's Bay?

The English named lots of places after explorers who sailed there. Vancouver's Island was named after Captain George Vancouver, and Hudson's Bay was named after Captain Henry Hudson. Later, the "s" at the end of these names was dropped. But by then, the Hudson's Bay Company was already named after the old "Hudson's Bay."

Actually, long before Hudson, there was already a Cree name for the bay: "wiinipaakw" or "winnipeg," meaning "nasty water"—probably because it was salty.

How many forts did the Hudson's Bay Company have?

The Hudson's Bay Company has been in business since 1614, longer than any other company in North America. It started with just one fort, Rupert House. Then a few more forts were built on the boggy, soggy shores of Hudson Bay—Moose Factory, York Factory, Albany, and Fort Prince of Wales. Cree traders with furs to sell made the long trek to the bay.

Then in the 1780s, a major rival, the North West Company, started building trading posts inland, closer to the fur supply. To make sure those Nor'westers didn't get all the furs, the Hudson's Bay Company was forced to build new trading posts. By 1800 there were 50, and by 1821 there were 154 (not including smaller outposts). That's the year the two companies merged into one, keeping the name Hudson's Bay Company. The company immediately fired staff and cut back the number of trading posts. By 1867, the year Canada became a country, there were 80 posts.

Do we have "Bog bodies" in our bogs?

No.

That's the short answer. I bet you have a long answer, too.

Of course. Hundreds of mysterious "bog bodies" were found in bogs in northern Europe. Some of these were thousands of years old but, like mummies, they were preserved in the bog environment. Most of these people had been killed and probably thrown into the bog as a human sacrifice. We've never found any bodies in our bogs here. At the time those bodies were thrown into European bogs, the aboriginal people living here in Canada weren't in the habit of chucking people into bogs.

MORTON'S IRRESISTIBLE DETOUR

Instead of "bog bodies," how about "glacier bodies?" Canada's glaciers are melting and uncovering things that have been frozen in ice for hundreds of years. In northern British Columbia, the remains of a 550-year-old man were found at the edge of the melting glacier. He probably died accidentally. He had a woven hat, a gopher-skin cloak, and a leather pouch filled with snacks of plants and fish. As glaciers continue to melt, maybe we'll find more glacier bodies—chilly links to the past.

This is hard work! We're not making much progress.

Maybe we're not paddling hard enough. Keep at it!

And More History

Are canoes originally from Canada?

No, canoes aren't really Canadian. Folks all over the world paddled canoes or canoe-like boats. The word "canoe" isn't Canadian, either. We got it from the French, who borrowed it from the Spanish, who probably heard it used hundreds of years ago by people living in the Caribbean and South America. It's a well-travelled word!

Canoes have become a Canadian symbol because they played such an important part in our history. Many different aboriginal groups had their own distinctive kinds of canoes. Canoes were then used by Europeans to explore inland Canada. Canoes were also the "freight trucks" of the fur trade, carrying loads across Canada's vast wilderness.

How did First Nations people hunt mammoths long ago?

Elephantlike mammoths with long, curly tusks roamed northern North America over 11,000 years ago. Prehistoric people living back then didn't have rifles for hunting, nor did they have bows and arrows. But they did have an accurate and powerful weapon—an atlatl. An atlatl could throw a metre-long (3-foot) spear or dart. It was a wooden stick about as long as two rulers end-to-end, with a handgrip at one end and a spur or bump sticking up at the other. The spear was placed along the atlatl with a notch at the end of the spear pushed up against the spur. The hunter would then swing the atlatl forward in a motion similar to an overhead tennis serve, launching the spear at a mammoth up to 100 metres (330 ft.) away!

Quick, Morton! It's charging!

Hmmm. I don't think my version of an atlatl really came out right.

Those mammoths were gigantic!

Indeed, mammoth-sized mammoths!

Ready to get dirty?
Is it absolutely necessary?
Archaeology involves digging in
the dirt. Also, sifting through old
garbage.
What fun.

Archaeological Adventures

Oldest evidence of human presence in North America!

What are some exciting archaeological discoveries in Canada?

Whoa, there's a lot of noise down below about the hot archaeological debate going on over the caves.

Archaeologists argue a lot over what happened in the human past, so they like finding clues that help piece together the puzzle. A lot of evidence is so old and open to different interpretations that there will always be debates over what the past can tell us.

Bluefish Caves

A group exploring the Bluefish River in northern Yukon accidentally discovered three limestone caves. The floor of the caves was covered with over a metre of dirt laid down, layer by layer, over 25,000 years. Archaeologists digging through this dirt found lots of animal bones. They also discovered a few stone tools used for scraping and cutting. Examining the bones under a microscope, they could see cut marks that appeared to have been made by humans butchering the animals.

When these butchered bones were dated to see how old they were, the archaeologists' jaws dropped. Although the dating is tricky, it appears that the bones were butchered between 10,000 and 25,000 years ago. One woolly mammoth bone showed marks where someone had chipped off flakes to make cutting tools 24,500 years ago!

What were humans doing in North America 24,500 years ago? (Eating supper, apparently.) The Bluefish Caves revealed the oldest evidence of humans ever found in North America.

Impossible! Those cave dates must be wrong. The first people reached North America about 12,000 years ago.

I agree. Our theory is that humans crossed a land bridge linking Russia and Alaska during the end of the last Ice Age. Then they migrated south along an ice-free corridor east of the Rocky Mountains.

Wait! They've found evidence that people were all the way down in Chile, South America, 12,500 years ago! That's *before* the date we're saying they crossed the land bridge to North America. The timing doesn't work.

Does that mean humans arrived in North America much earlier than we thought — as the evidence found in the Bluefish Caves indicates?

But even if we accept the Bluefish evidence, how would those early people travel south? North America was covered in ice sheets back then.

Along the Pacific coast, perhaps? Hopping from island to island in boats? There might have been spots that were ice-free.

But the sea level has risen since then, so any evidence of people along the coast would now be underwater.

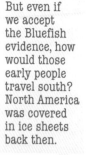

To be continued …

A lot of buffaloes went over the cliff!

There were lots, back then. The Blackfoot used the animals for food, clothing, shelter, and tools.

One of world's oldest and best-preserved buffalo jumps.

Head-Smashed-In Buffalo Jump

Stand clear! Stampeding buffalo thunder across the grasslands. Hunters circling behind and upwind of the herd scare the animals into panic by shouting and waving robes. V-shaped drive lanes lined with piles of stones help funnel the buffalo towards the cliff kill site. Those in the lead are pushed over the cliff by those behind. The heavy beasts plummet 30 metres (100 ft.) to the ground below, where Native hunters stand ready with lance, club, or bow and arrow to finish them off.... This jump in southern Alberta was used for over 5,700 years, until the mid-1800s. When it was excavated in 1938, the pile of buffalo bones and dirt was over 10 metres (33 ft.) thick.

Site of earliest-known European settlement in North America.

L'Anse aux Meadows

Grassy mounds rising out of a meadow on the northern tip of Newfoundland. Archaeologists looking at this site in 1960 thought these mounds seemed to form faint rectangular outlines. When they started digging, they uncovered remnants of the walls of large, sod-covered houses.

Amazingly, they had unearthed a thousand-year-old Norse settlement, complete with a large hall, workshops, a fireplace, a cooking pit, and a smithy for mending iron tools. The settlement would have only been occupied for a few years before its Norse residents (sometimes known as Vikings) returned home to Greenland. L'Anse aux Meadows is the oldest-known European settlement in North America, occupied 500 years before Christopher Columbus sailed to America.

Was this place Vinland, the legendary land mentioned in the Norse Sagas written 1,000 years ago?

Maybe; maybe not. We can't really say.

That's not helpful.

That's life sometimes.

Is it OK to eat Canadian snow?

Stick to just a flake or two. Snowflake crystals actually form on small pieces of dust—then pick up pollution from the air as they fall from the clouds.

Digging into Food

Why are Saskatoon berries blue?

I think Saskatoon berries are actually purple not blue.

It's a really deep, dark blue. A purplish blue.

Or a bluish purple.

Saskatoon berries are blue because they contain pigments called anthocyanins. Anthocyanins give fruits and vegetables their colour. They not only turn Saskatoon berries blue, they're also good for your health.

TODAY'S SPECIAL: SASKATOON BERRY PIE

Saskatoon berries

MORTON'S IRRESISTIBLE DETOUR

The Cree, who ate lots of Saskatoon berries, called them *missaskquatoomina*. (Look closely—the origin of the word "Saskatoon" is in there somewhere.) The berries were mushed up with fat and dried meat to make pemmican— early energy food. Frankly, it was the berries that made the pemmican edible.

How did the chokecherry get its name?

Ever eaten chokecherries? If you have, you'll understand the name. The wild black cherries are so bitter and sour you'll want to choke!

Hint: When you dry chokecherries or make them into jelly, the acidic taste goes away. That's no choke!...er... I mean, no joke!

Chokecherries

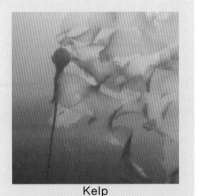

Kelp

Irish moss

How many types of seaweed can you eat?

You *can* eat any seaweed, since none are poisonous. Hey—I didn't say you'd like them all but they are packed with healthy nutrients.

Though in Asian countries people gobble up a wide variety of seaweeds in soups, salads, and sashimi garnishes, Canada hasn't caught on to the idea of seaweed as a culinary delight.

One seaweed that's eaten as a snack in Atlantic Canada is dulse. It's collected at low tide and dried in the sun. You could start your seaweed snacking with dulse, and once you're a seaweed fan, try some of the others: a little sea lettuce in a salad, some kelp or rockweed in your chowder, or some Irish moss to help thicken your soup.

Where does maple syrup come from?

What a sweet question!
Actually, it's a little sappy.

In spring, when the weather gets warmer, the sap starts to run inside sugar maple and red maple trees. A hole is drilled into the trunk, a spout is banged into the opening, and the sap that drips out is collected into a bucket or runs into a tube. The sap is then boiled until the water evaporates and the syrup becomes thick and sweet. It takes about 40 litres (10 1/2 gallons) of sap to produce a single litre (about 1/4 gallon) of maple syrup.

Interview with Diane Bernard, a.k.a. "The Seaweed Lady."

Vivien: What's so wonderful about seaweed?

Diane Bernard: Seaweeds are the healthiest plants on the planet! And delicious, with so many tastes, textures, and flavours. They grow wild along our coastlines. There are 250 varieties of seaweed just in the small area where I harvest. Canadians don't value their wild seaweed enough.

Vivien: Maybe that's because seaweed stinks?

Diane Bernard: Nonsense! Fresh seaweed tastes like a vegetable without the fishy smell. You're thinking of the piles of rotting seaweed on the beach. Step over them and go down to low tide. There you'll find the wildest, fastest-growing, and most exotic garden in the world. I deliver fresh seaweed to some very fancy restaurants, where chefs have concocted fabulous seaweed cuisine. I also take people on seaweed tours, so they can crunch and lunch on different varieties.

Vivien: Seaweeds: the food of the future?

Diane Bernard: Excuse me, I have to go. The tide is going out and....

Vivien: It's seaweed harvesting time! I understand.

Diane Bernard

93

Acknowledgements

One of the delights of writing this book was tapping into the brains of knowledgeable people from many different fields. Thanks for your help: Maureen Anderson, German speaker; Robert Anderson, Canadian Museum of Nature; Peter & Barbara Barham, penguin researchers; Diane Bernard, Outercoast Seaweeds; Sharon T. Brown, biologist; Dr. Stephen Bruneau, iceberg expert; Ken Burton, National Wildlife Federation; Andrew A. Bryant, Vancouver Island Marmot Foundation; Jacques Cinq-Mars, archaeologist; Vince Crichton, Manitoba Wildlife and Ecosystem Protection Branch; Doug Currie, Royal Ontario Museum; Randall Dibblee, Wildlife Biologist, P.E.I. Dept. of Environment & Energy; Robert Forsyth, Research Associate, Royal B.C. Museum; Robert Geldart, City of Edmonton; Doug Hallman, Sudbury Neutrino Observatory; Steve Herrero, University of Calgary; Gord Kijek, Alberta Infrastructure & Transportation; Hans Larsson, Canada Research Chair in Vertebrate Palaeontology, McGill University; Ty Eng Lim, Education Coordinator, GagiNang; Roy MacGregor, author; Ian Macek, firefighter; Peter Macek, science instructor; Dr.Eric Mattson, Chair, Dept. of Geography and Geology, Nipissing University; David Mitchell, chemist; Paul Moisson, firefighter; Moose Foundation; Reza Moridi, Radiation Safety Institute of Canada; David Morrison, Archaeological Survey of Canada; Anthony (Tony) L. Nette, Manager, Wildlife Resources, Nova Scotia; Michael Naab, Director, Ketchikan Museums; Donna Naughton, Canadian Museum of Nature; Heather Pitcher, Hudson's Bay Company Archives; Brian Port, Canadian Hydrographic Service; Kim Poole, wildlife biologist; Harry Quesnel, plant ecologist; David B. Richman, entomologist; Avalon Smith, principal, Umimmak School, Grise Fiord; Dan Spivak, Royal Tyrrell Museum; Dr. Ian Stirling, Canadian Wildlife Service; John Tarduno, University of Rochester; Brian Terry/Leah Seaman, Inuvik residents; Glen Wright, National Archives of Canada

And, of course, thanks to all the kids whose questions were used in Crazy About Canada:

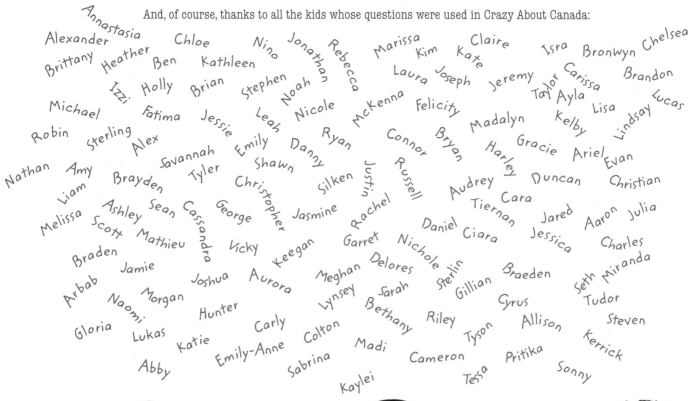

Annastasia, Alexander, Chloe, Nino, Jonathan, Rebecca, Marissa, Kim, Kate, Claire, Isra, Bronwyn, Chelsea, Brittany, Heather, Ben, Kathleen, Laura, Joseph, Jeremy, Carissa, Brandon, Izzi, Holly, Brian, Stephen, Noah, Taylor, Ayla, Lisa, Lucas, Michael, Fatima, Jessie, Leah, Nicole, McKenna, Felicity, Madalyn, Kelby, Lindsay, Robin, Sterling, Alex, Emily, Ryan, Connor, Bryan, Gracie, Ariel, Evan, Nathan, Amy, Savannah, Tyler, Shawn, Danny, Silken, Justin, Russell, Harley, Duncan, Christian, Liam, Brayden, Sean, Christopher, Jasmine, Rachel, Audrey, Cara, Jared, Aaron, Julia, Melissa, Ashley, Cassandra, George, Keegan, Garret, Nichole, Tiernan, Jessica, Charles, Scott, Mathieu, Vicky, Daniel, Ciara, Seth, Miranda, Braden, Jamie, Joshua, Aurora, Meghan, Delores, Sterlin, Braeden, Arbab, Morgan, Lynsey, Sarah, Gillian, Cyrus, Tudor, Naomi, Hunter, Bethany, Riley, Allison, Steven, Gloria, Lukas, Katie, Carly, Colton, Madi, Tyson, Kerrick, Abby, Emily-Anne, Sabrina, Cameron, Pritika, Sonny, Kaylei, Tessa

94

Photo Credits

Care has been taken to trace ownership of copyright materials contained in this book. Information enabling the publisher to rectify any reference or credit line in future editions will be welcomed.

For reasons of space, the following abbreviations have been used:

DT: Dave Taylor, Senses of Wilderness Inc.

LP: Lone Pine Photo

RB: Robert Berdan, Science & Art Multimedia

VP: Valan Photos

Index

Page numbers in italics refer to illustrations.